RIGHT
NOW
LEADERSHIP

A 4-Part Framework for Today's Leaders

Written by
Kyle Gillette

https://www.blueshirtcoaching.com

Skinny Brown Dog Media

🌐 www.SkinnyBrownDogMedia.com

Published by Skinny Brown Dog Media
Atlanta, GA/Punta del Este, Uruguay

🌐 http://www.SkinnyBrownDogMedia.com

Distributed by Skinny Brown Dog Media
Design and composition by Skinny Brown Dog Media
Cover Design by Skinny Brown Dog Media
Cover Design by Skinny Brown Dog Media

Library of Congress Cataloging-in-Publication Data Print

eBook ISBN: 978-1-957506-68-5
Hardback ISBN: 978-1-957506-69-2
Paperback ISBN: 978-1-957506-70-8
Case Laminate ISBN: 978-1-957506-71-5

Acknowledgments

I would like to thank my wife, Kari Gillette, for sticking with me through this process, editing the first drafts, and continuing to help me refine and adjust the book.

Thank you to my editor Eric Reid for making this process smooth, professional, and fun.

Thank you to Alex Hall, Anita Galliford, Charles Molenkamp, Shay Niewiadomski, and Richard Leong for being my first readers and giving me invaluable feedback on the rough, rough draft.

Contents

Introduction:

The BLUE Shirt Leadership and the Big Bad Wolf

Once upon a time, there were three little pigs. The first pig built his house with straw, the second with sticks, and the third built his home out of bricks.

A big bad wolf watched the little pigs while they danced and played and thought, "What juicy, tender meals they will make!" They ran and hid in their houses as he began to hunt the pigs.

Standing in front of the house made of straw, he huffed and puffed and blew the house down. The frightened little pig ran to the second pig's house, made of sticks. The big bad wolf, unwilling to give up a good juicy meal, approached the second house, huffed, puffed, and blew the stick house down. Now, the two little pigs were terrified and ran to the house of the third pig, who had taken the time to build his home out of bricks.

Still determined to get his meal of fresh, juicy piglet, the big bad wolf stood in front of the brick house, and he huffed and puffed, but he could not blow the house down. He kept trying for hours, but the house would not fall. The little pigs were safe inside thanks to the hard work of the wise pig who had taken the time to build his brick house.

After the wolf had given up and gone home, the two little pigs built their houses with bricks, and all three of the pigs lived happily ever after.

Your Leadership House

What does the story of the three little pigs have to do with your leadership and business future? A LOT. I'm not implying which of the three pigs you might be, but I know which of three pigs a BLUE Shirt Leader would be!

To explain the BLUE Shirt Leadership Framework, picture your leadership as a house built over time and with intention.

Be a Self-Aware Leader serves as the foundation of your leadership house (and your business). The more self-aware you are, the stronger your foundation will be. A foundation of self-awareness has a broad base to make your impact as a leader.

Lead with Accountability represents the nails in your leadership house. Without accountability, your home would come crumbling down. Sometimes these nails begin to loosen, and you must take out your hammer and nail them back in. Other times, you may not notice the nails popping until someone hands you the hammer and points out the work to be done.

Use a Growth Mindset is represented by the walls and roof of your leadership house. As you grow in your leadership abilities and experience, the structure of your house will be remodeled to accommodate the people under your roof. Your growth needs to be properly supported with a strong foundation.

Working together, self-awareness and growth provide more opportunities to influence those you lead in meaningful ways.

Empower Others serves as the windows and doors to your leadership house. It is how people see opportunities to branch out on their own. The windows and doors give them a view of what is possible and a way to move on to new opportunities.

Furthermore, the windows and doors provide opportunities for others to observe and eventually join what you are doing.

Think about your leadership house for a moment.

- How strong is your foundation?
- How secure are those nails?
- How high is the roof to your leadership?
- How many people enjoy being in your house?

In the tale of the three little pigs, the story's moral is about each pig's actions, his work ethic and habits, and the impact those actions had. Each house the pigs constructed reflected their character. Your habits and mindsets determine the quality of your BLUE Shirt Leadership house.

The big bad wolf in our entrepreneurial journey represents the problems, bad habits, distractions, etc., that can disrupt your leadership. If you aren't mindful, your leadership house could start to fall.

Like most children's stories written to teach us something, the story of the three pigs ends on a happy note. Similarly, as you get your leadership house in order using the power of the BLUE Shirt Leadership Framework, the big bad wolf of challenges comes and tries to blow your leadership house down, but he will only rattle the windows or may cause some external damage. He may even get into your home, but you'll be ready to flush out and resolve whatever the "wolf" is in your leadership.

The beauty of the BLUE Shirt Leadership Framework is that all four pillars work together to build a strong leadership house that will withstand the external and internal factors that can collapse some leaders. The habits and mindsets will reinforce your foundation of self-awareness taught in this book. The nails of accountability become more effective, and the hammer of accountability is ready as you leverage the strategies mentioned in this book.

As you grow as a leader, you may, from time to time, decide to remodel your leadership house to accommodate new abilities and those you lead. The windows and doors become more inviting and light up your home for people to enjoy what it's like to be led by you. The windows and doors also are open for those you lead to step away and pass on what they have learned to others.

■ What To Expect

If you are ready to find confidence and clarity in your leadership, this book will give you the framework to do it.

When you read this book, you will learn how to lead like the best leaders. Discover how to be a great leader to change your company culture, grow your business, develop people to their full potential and live a life with meaning.

This book is for you if you're a business owner who wants to leave a legacy. With BLUE Shirt Leadership, you will learn the behaviors, thinking patterns, and consistency needed to become the leader you're meant to be.

The BLUE Shirt Leadership Framework has four pillars to help build lasting leadership changes. For a simple guy like me, I love to use acronyms and this framework is easily summarized in the acronym B.L.U.E. This is why my business is called BLUE Shirt Coaching. We have to put on this framework every day. The framework pillars are creating a mindset of self-awareness, building a network of accountability, mastering the growth mindset, and leveraging your ability to empower others. Within each pillar, there are five mindsets and habits.

As you build these pillars, you'll find that your mindset shifts to being more passionate and more intentional about the contributions you make. Your empowerment of others will deepen their growth as leaders and, in turn, your growth as a leader.

You'll develop grit and become more hardworking. Your goal will be to create an environment where everyone can excel and do their best work while achieving true leadership greatness.

Ultimately, leadership is about clarifying your vision, values, mindsets, and habits, then establishing patterns that embody these pieces. How this is achieved is not a one-size-fits-all solution. While there might be some universal truths to leadership, every person has their own story. This book provides a framework for how you can write your leadership story as you build your BLUE Shirt Leadership house.

The Four Pillars of the BLUE Shirt Leadership Framework are:

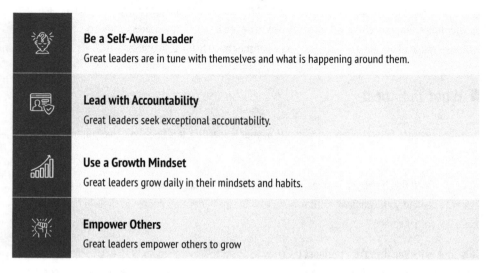

Be a Self-Aware Leader
Great leaders are in tune with themselves and what is happening around them.

Lead with Accountability
Great leaders seek exceptional accountability.

Use a Growth Mindset
Great leaders grow daily in their mindsets and habits.

Empower Others
Great leaders empower others to grow

Now is the time to become a BLUE Shirt Leader. When you implement the BLUE Shirt Leadership Framework, you will feel more fulfilled as a leader, your stress will decrease, and you will look forward to the future of your business. No longer will you feel overwhelmed, unfulfilled, and unmotivated.

Who Is This Book For?

- ☑ Small business owners seeking to grow their businesses through great leadership and their team
- ☑ Small business owners who are currently in transition and want to see significant growth
- ☑ Business owners struggling to find clarity of vision and certainty in their business
- ☑ Business leaders who want strong teams
- ☑ Business owners who want predictable growth in their leadership

The framework in this book guarantees professional and personal growth.

If you want to see things differently and not stay stuck in your head, this book will help you. Your mindsets and habits are the keys to getting what you desire. The BLUE Shirt Leadership Framework makes this possible.

A Motorcycle Accident That Shifted My Life

In 2008 I was in a motorcycle accident that nearly took my life. Having been riding motorcycles for two years, I was getting a little overconfident. I'd take my Harley Sportster out with friends around Lopez Lake in San Luis Obispo County. It's a fun, curvy, and hilly road to ride and has great views.

A few of my friends had sports bikes—watching them lay their bikes low challenged me to do the same. I got so good at it that I remember pulling over to the side and showing my friends how the foot peg had scraped the road. I still can't believe I rode like that on a Sportster!

After being able to ride aggressively, I seized on an opportunity to go for a ride up in the hills around the Pismo Beach area. I found a new housing development area overlooking the Pacific Ocean with excellent, newly paved roads, but no construction had begun. That morning when I rode out, I had no idea how much this ride would change my life.

The roads were perfect. There was no shoulder to the road, just asphalt up to raised curbs. It was a gorgeous morning, with no one around. So, I gunned it.

The development was a curvy road in the middle of hilly pastureland that ended in a large cul-de-sac. After a few blissful moments of enjoying the view from the end of the development, I put my helmet back on and gunned it to get back home.

Heading up a hill, I'd forgotten it turned sharply just before the crest. My speedometer read 50 miles per hour when I saw the curve in the road. Instead of leaning the bike hard, I panicked and locked up both brakes.

The motorcycle's wheels locked up and began to slide. I remember looking at the speedometer as all this was going on, and it read 30 miles per hour. Then BAM! The front tire hit the curb, launching me off the bike. When I came to, with my legs tangled in a barbed-wire fence, I realized that I had flown over thirty feet in the air.

After untangling my legs and sitting up, I could see the motorcycle was less than eighteen inches from my head. The bike would have smashed my skull if my legs had not gotten caught in the barbed wire fence.

I got a concussion and still have the scars on my shin from getting caught in the fence. But I was alive.

That day, God spared my life. He had chosen not just to spare my life but to allow me to walk away. That day revealed a deeper purpose for my life than I was living for at the time.

This new awareness is the heart behind the creation of BLUE Shirt Coaching and the BLUE Shirt Leadership Framework. This accident created a change in my heart and mind that has driven me to help others live their lives on purpose and purposefully. I promise that the BLUE Shirt Leadership Framework will help you be a self-aware leader you are meant to be. I was not that leader the day of my accident, but each day after, I have focused on becoming the leader I am meant to be.

The BLUE Shirt Leadership Framework is my way of growing entrepreneur leaders. Entrepreneurs are some of the most influential people in the world. Without the work your company does, our world would look very different. The actions you take after learning this framework will be part of the legacy of my life being spared that day in 2008. But there's more to the story of how BLUE Shirt Coaching and the leadership framework came to exist. It wasn't my idea.

The Voice at 3:00 a.m.

We've all been there: awake at 3:00 a.m. and unable to get a stupid thought to leave your mind. You know you must do something with that thought. Maybe you keep a notepad on your nightstand, or your phone sits nearby on the dresser. You tell yourself, "I need to get up and get this out of my head."

This happened to me a few years ago. For weeks, I'd been working on developing a phrase for leadership. The goal of the framework I was searching for was to improve my leadership and help others lead in better ways.

At 3:00 a.m., I shot bolt-upright in bed after hearing the word "self-awareness." It felt like God had given me the missing word of the framework I had been working on for months.

I jumped out of bed and ran to the kitchen. While sitting there shivering in my boxers over the next four hours, I downloaded the beginnings of the BLUE Shirt Leadership Framework. The voice I heard at 3:00 a.m. was the catalyst to the BLUE Shirt Leadership Framework and this book, course, and app.

The word "self-awareness" was the key. I had already begun thinking about accountability, development, empowerment, support, etc., but they were missing something. The self-awareness piece is what was able to form the foundation of the framework. Without self-awareness, accountability, growth and empowerment aren't nearly as powerful.,

The framework was born, and I was empowered. Sometimes all we need is a word to shift our lives and businesses in unique ways. This book will be that shift for you.

As I continued to research and work with this framework, it became clear that if you take any successful person in history, you could find the BLUE Shirt Leadership Framework behind that success.

All highly successful business owners, influencers, moms, spouses, athletes, and musicians have something in common: their mindset. Whether they know they have what I call the BLUE Shirt Leadership Mindset or not, the evidence exists in their life, and it's changed the lives of everyone around them.

■ Where Are You on Your Journey?

- ☑ Do you feel like you are the only one who knows how to do the job right?
- ☑ Do you feel like you are on the edge of something huge but just can't get the time to make it happen?
- ☑ Do you have great ideas, but they're not coming together?
- ☑ Do you want more confidence and clarity in how to lead?
- ☑ Are you tired of second-guessing yourself and playing small?
- ☑ Do you want people around you to follow, respect, and trust you?

If you answer yes to any of these questions, I know you are not alone, and this book will give you the framework to break through many of the entrepreneurial and leadership traps, pitfalls, and limitations you've fallen victim to.

Skeptics, Read This

You may wonder if this is just another one of those self-serving, fluff-filled, self-help books—and that's okay! I get it. I promise you that this book will help you. The teaching and lessons will get into your head and help you make fundamental shifts that stick.

How This Book Is Different

This book is different because it provides a simple and memorable framework for you to develop your leadership greatness around. In this book, you'll learn practical and valuable terms, processes, and questions to help you APPLY the BLUE Shirt Leadership Framework.

Through the practical tools created as part of the BLUE Shirt Leadership Framework, you can access a community of growing leaders and a 40+ video training course to develop your BLUE Shirt Leadership Mindset. I have BLUE Shirt Leadership masterminds and coaching programs that connect you with like-minded business owners to help you grow and apply these principles.

Business owners and leaders need concrete and practical strategies to manage their business and effectively lead. This book is about helping you make small mindset and habit shifts daily that will bring about massive results for the rest of your life and career.

■ How To Read This Book

I suggest you read this book with pen and paper or a notes app in hand. As you read, keep an eye out for questions in each chapter. Look for sections that encourage you to stop and take notes. Taking notes will help you slow down and reflect on what you are learning and how to apply what you're learning to your life.

To get the most out of this book, read in twenty-five-minute increments. Studies show that our brains do best with twenty-five-minute or shorter learning intervals. There is no need to rush through this book. Each time you sit down to read, ask yourself two primary questions:

What am I hoping to learn from this book?

⮕ What am I going to do with what I learn?

The goal is for you to shift and grow in ten to twelve mindsets and habits you learn from this book. You'll be amazed at how it takes only ten to fifteen minutes a day to experience serious shifts in your leadership.

As you work on the mindsets and habits in this book, note areas you may struggle with. Second, note the areas that you feel very confident about. This way, you can quickly scan your notes and find in which areas you are doing well. Focusing on strengths has proven in study after study to be the best way to improve leadership and performance.

■ The Speed-Reading Program

In the 1950s, the Nebraska School Study Council supported a statewide research project on teaching speed reading. About six thousand tenth graders participated in the study, with the average student reading about 90 words per minute. After the program, these same students averaged 150 words per minute—a 60 percent improvement.

Some naturally talented readers went through the program. These readers averaged about 300 words per minute. After the program, they were averaging a staggering 2,900 words per minute!

This statewide study is interesting because it emphasizes the importance of focusing on natural talents and strengths. Similarly, this book focuses you on your natural mindsets and habits. The greatest gift you can give yourself as you read this book is to set your mind on choosing the attitudes and practices you are great at, then finding people or systems to manage the rest.

At the end of this book, you will develop your own BLUE Shirt Leadership Plan to shift your behaviors and mindset to equip you with all the tools needed to become the leader you're meant to be!

In the next chapter, we'll look at some of the "big bad wolf's" tricks to try to blow down your leadership house.

Chapter 1:

The Small Business Owner Struggle

A popular speaker started a seminar by holding up a twenty-dollar bill. A crowd of two hundred had gathered to hear him speak that day. He asked, "Who would like this twenty-dollar bill?"

Several hands went up.

He said, "I will give this twenty-dollar bill to one of you, but first, let me do this." He crumpled the bill up.

He then asked, "Who still wants it?" The same hands rose.

"Well," he replied, "What if I do this?" Then he dropped the twenty-dollar bill on the ground and stomped on it with his shoes.

He picked it up and showed it to the crowd. The bill was all crumpled and dirty. "Now, who still wants it?" The same hands went up.

"My friends, I have just shown you a critical lesson. No matter what I did to the money, you still wanted it because its value did not change in your eyes. To you, it was still worth twenty dollars."

Life crumples us and grinds us into the dirt. We make bad decisions or end up in poor circumstances. Sometimes we can feel worthless, broken, and collapsed. But no matter what has happened or will happen, you will never lose your value. You are special—don't ever forget it!

Remember this twenty-dollar bill when the big bad wolf comes to knock you or your business down. When you finish this book, you will have an excellent grasp of what is possible for your leadership and the value you bring.

The Struggles of Business Leaders

Leaders struggle daily with a lack of motivation, working long hours, and feeling overworked. Some also feel a lack of confidence in themselves or their team. They feel like imposters as leaders. Additionally, they struggle to avoid burnout from all the hard work it takes to complete their daily responsibilities.

Today's leadership requires constantly having to make tough decisions to meet demands. With these difficulties come lower satisfaction levels among leaders and higher rates of dissatisfied employees within organizations. High turnover and an unstable leadership team contribute to daily struggles for business owners like you.

By now, as a small business owner and leader, you understand how much responsibility is on your shoulders. As the leader of your company, you often have as many, if not more, obligations as other leaders. You are in a position where no one is around to lean on or look over your shoulder to help make decisions when things get tough.

It seems like each day, more and more gets piled on top of the previous day's work, much of which appears to have URGENT or PAST DUE stamped on it! With so many responsibilities on your plate, it is understandable to feel you don't have a solid grasp of them all. Amidst all you must do, you are required to give guidance and support to so many different people that it can feel like the whole world is relying on just one person: YOU.

In this chapter, I want to share what I believe the big bad wolf of leadership is using to try to knock you down:

- Overworked and overwhelmed – Busyness
- Lack of time – Priority challenges
- Low confidence – Imposter Syndrome
- Inconsistent actions – Accountability
- No vision – Surviving

Overworked and Overwhelmed

For about six months in 2015, I was an executive director at a senior living facility. This facility was part of a large, multi-location company with all the stereotypical trappings of a bad corporate bureaucracy.

The residents and my coworkers were fantastic. However, the corporate management was harsh on our team, forcing us to work long, unproductive hours and labeling us as failures. Any suggestions for improvements or changes that we made were ignored. The company's primary focus was profit.

Our mission statement could have been "Figure out how to make more spend less." Not a bad goal on its own, right? However, the corporate management was so focused on this single goal that they overlooked how hard we, their employees, were working, how much we cared about the residents that called the living facility home, and how overworked and overwhelmed we were becoming.

My leadership contributions to this company didn't make a difference to management. After six challenging and unrewarding months, I decided to leave the company. It was nearly impossible to be productive and make a difference in such a toxic environment.

Yes, I was part of a large corporation, but it's just as easy to feel overworked and overwhelmed in a small business, especially when you are in charge.

The job expectations increase while the allotted time and available resources decrease.

Old problems keep resurfacing despite your best efforts to avoid them.

You feel like there is so much to do and too little time to do it.

Your workload is unevenly distributed throughout the year.

Besides the pressures of running your business, you also have personal goals and aspirations. You feel so overwhelmed by the demands of your business that you can never dedicate any time to your personal life.

You need to face these challenges now.

You must get a handle on this right now because your business's success depends on it. The bottom line is that leaders who are overworked and overwhelmed aren't very effective.

If you are experiencing any of this, now is the time to do something about it. Exceptional leaders understand how to manage their time and can complete things other managers only fantasize about.

They have a system that allows them to accomplish more with their time than others in similar positions. In part, they've prioritized figuring out what works for them and sticking with it.

Shifting toward a BLUE Shirt Leadership Mindset will be exponentially challenging if you can't get your time under control. While this isn't a book on time management, sometimes a few tweaks here and there to your mindset and behaviors create the shifts necessary to gain control of your time and become a BLUE Shirt Leader.

For small business owners, time seems to have a way of escaping your grasp when you reach for it. You'll often work around the clock to keep up with never-ending demands.

Just like building a home takes months of preparation, construction, and detailed touches before you can move in, building a BLUE Shirt Leadership House does too. Leverage every moment you have to build that BLUE Shirt Leadership House, and you'll make progress. Here are three strategies to help you get started.

The Time Account

Imagine you have a bank account that receives and automatically deposits $86,400 each morning. The account does not carry over a balance from day to day. Every night, whatever part of the automatic deposit that is unused is returned. What would you do? I know I would spend every dollar I could every day!

We all have such a bank account.

Every morning, you have 86,400 seconds deposited into your life. Every day, you lose whatever time you don't intentionally use. You can't keep a balance of unused minutes on your account. The account starts fresh every day and returns any unused time at the end of the day.

Oh, and the truth is there is never any borrowing of time. You can't take a loan on your time or against someone else's. The time you have is the time you have, and that is that. We have the same amount each day as everyone else. The problem is that it's easy not to prioritize this limited resource well.

What's the strategy for success here? First, understand that once something is measured, it becomes much easier to improve. The challenge is that most people don't accurately measure their current time management skills. Here are methods to help you capture your time more effectively.

■ Three Ways to Retake Control of Your Time:

- ⊃ The Pomodoro technique
- ⊃ Eat That Frog
- ⊃ The Two-Minute Rule

■ The Pomodoro Technique

Knowing where your time goes makes it easier to have a productive day!

The Pomodoro technique is a time management method developed in the late 1980s by Francesco Cirillo. It uses a timer to break down your work into intervals (called "Pomodoro's") separated by short breaks.

This is the method behind the recommended ten- to twenty-five-minute reading intervals.

STEP 1
Decide on the tasks you want to accomplish.

STEP2
Set a timer for twenty-five minutes. Make sure it is visible.

STEP 3
Take a five-minute break.

STEP 4
Repeat three to six times throughout the day.

Keep doing only the task at hand until the timer rings, signaling a change in focus.

■ Eat That Frog

Mark Twain said, "Eat a live frog the first thing in the morning, and nothing worse will happen to you the rest of the day." What does this mean for productivity?

B.L.U.E Shirt Leadership Framework

Make your frog your most difficult and important task—the one you will procrastinate on unless you do something about it. Doing this task and getting it out of the way will make the rest of the tasks seem easy by comparison.

Finishing this item on your to-do list is a huge accomplishment and will give you the momentum you need to complete other tasks.

■ The Two-Minute Rule

This rule is a quick way to overcome procrastination or low motivation. It is based on the philosophy that we can do anything for two minutes. By setting a timer for two-minute increments, you are making small, manageable steps toward the long-term goal you have set for yourself.

This rule will also help you quickly work through all the simple, short tasks and get them off your list so you can focus on the most important. If it takes two minutes or less, do it. Then move on.

As in leadership, time management requires a unique combination of skills, intuition, and persistence. You'll find you're already using some of these techniques and many others, but when you become more intentional with your time, those 86,400 seconds seem a lot more valuable.

Feeling Like an Imposter

When I started my coaching and consulting practice, I had an opportunity to work with a company in the energy sector. It was a whale of a client and my very first one.

The contract provided DISC assessments (a behavioral assessment tool) and workshops to the branch's VP and team. In saying yes, I stepped into what would be a huge learning experience.

Every team member received an assessment and review. The assessment process went relatively smoothly, and the debrief conversations were helpful. But in the strategy meeting, things got uncomfortable.

I was sitting in a fancy boardroom with three team members on the phone, including the VP and three other team members. I was at the head of the table, trying to engage the group in conversation.

No one was engaging, responses were short, and the VP showed zero signs of providing me a lifeline. Eventually, the administrative lady (thank goodness for her) stepped in and started sharing her thoughts and perspective.

After ninety minutes of fits and starts, the whole thing was over. I briefly chatted with the VP and other team members before leaving. The VP said I'd done a good job, but it felt like a platitude, and I left feeling like a complete fraud.

Many small business owners have had this experience in sales meetings, in boardrooms, and in front of their employees. There's nothing like standing in front of a group and feeling like you shouldn't be there.

Improving Your Confidence

The first step in improving your confidence as a leader is acknowledging why it may be lacking. Maybe you don't see yourself as effective with your current leadership skills, or perhaps you lack self-confidence because you haven't pushed for the opportunity to grow in your current role.

Maybe you lack confidence because you aren't consistently practicing self-development activities to help you with your knowledge and proficiency. If this is the case, you can turn things around by scheduling time each day to work on a specific development activity related to your leadership skills.

It can be tricky to find a plan or process to help you improve your confidence, but it's not impossible. Here are some options to consider:

- Join a networking group in person (or online).
- Find a mastermind group.
- Get in front of a camera or onto a podcast.
- Start looking for speaking engagements.
- Join Toastmasters© to practice public speaking.
- Practice the mindfulness tactics taught in this book.

Experiment with various options until you find something that resonates with your interests. You will not gain confidence by only reading books and watching videos. You need to push yourself and believe in yourself. Act "as if" you already have the confidence. Through a combination of taking action, moving outside your comfort zone, and being mindful of the imposter and confidence feelings, you will experience growth in these areas.

Once you've discovered a few activities that get you excited about growing and improving your confidence, the next step is making time to practice these skills. Schedule them in your daily or weekly calendar to ensure they happen.

■ Build a Better System

While these are practical things you can and should do, there's a secret to this imposter issue. It's a secret a client recently discovered.

I asked Joe, "When do you feel like an imposter?" He responded, "When I'm thinking about what result I could produce for the prospect."

I said, "How's your confidence when you are in the sales conversation or networking with prospects?" Joe responded, "I feel good. I know what I'm talking about." He seemed only to have an imposter mindset when producing what he said he could do.

The coaching call continued with a discussion about where the imposter's feeling was coming from. For Joe, it wasn't in people's interactions but rather the unknown outcome of the process he led his client through.

Through coaching, Joe realized the problem was in the reliability of his system, not in his ability to achieve results. He knew if he put the work into developing a clear, repeatable system, this would help him have the right mindset about his abilities, and his confidence would grow. Having a system to achieve results, achieving the results the system was designed for, and being able to repeat the system over and over is a beautiful feedback loop.

My client became self-aware of the broken mindset. He saw the growth opportunity was to improve his system. In other words, he knew it would work and believed in himself and the process. This gave him genuine confidence.

The accountability comes from the new system and the important question we helped create. The coaching helped empower him to make critical shifts, opening the door to new opportunities and winning him a $50,000 contract.

Changing mindsets and systems is critical for building confidence and breaking imposter patterns. Together we will dive deeper into the systems and mindset in chapter 5.

■ Questions To Ponder

➲ What three qualities do you need to be more confident?

➲ What would it look like to develop these qualities?

➲ What would it feel like once they were developed?

These questions allow you to create your ideal future and get your unconscious working on the problem-solving to make it happen. When you can see what you want to become, new possibilities are available to you, and shifts will follow.

Take your time to review the questions above and write your responses in your notes.

With a Great Vision Comes the Need for Great Commitment and Consistency

A man was broke and living in a tiny house, with only a beat-up car to his name. He was living off a $99 monthly government check. At sixty-five years of age, he decided things had to change. So, he thought about what he had to offer. His friends raved about his chicken recipe. He agreed that his chicken was the best and decided that starting a chicken business was his best shot at making a change.

He left Kentucky and traveled to different states to sell his recipe. He told restaurant owners that he had a mouthwatering chicken recipe. He offered the recipe for free and asked for a small percentage of the chicken they sold from using his recipe. It sounds like a good deal, right?

Unfortunately, not to most of the restaurant owners. The man heard NO over a thousand times. He continued to believe his chicken recipe was special, even with a thousand rejections. Despite the rejections, he didn't give up.

On the 1,010th try, he finally received his first YES. Colonel Hartland Sanders changed how Americans eat chicken. Kentucky Fried Chicken, popularly known as KFC, was born.

Colonel Sanders had a great vision. He was so clear and committed to it that he could withstand rejection over a thousand times.

How often does the average person give up after being rejected: once or twice? Far too many.

To have any hope of fulfilling your vision, commitment to it and communication about it are critical. Colonel Sanders believed in his recipe and himself. He demonstrated an unwavering belief in the dream he had. Frustration develops when we don't live out our vision.

Communicating your vision clearly and authentically and speaking simply and precisely about what you stand for makes it much easier for people to follow your dream and say yes. Colonel Sanders had a thousand opportunities to communicate his vision. Someone caught his vision and said yes on that one thousand and tenth time he shared the dream.

When you are unclear about your vision and messages, people have difficulty buying into it and supporting you. If this happens, there's a severe impact on your ability to deliver value. It drives people away from you and causes some who previously believed in you to look for other options.

In chapters 3 and 8, this book outlines a process to determine your values and vision.

■ Questions To Ponder

- ⮑ What is one thing you would do if you knew that nothing would hold you back?
- ⮑ What would you do if you knew there were no limitations?
- ⮑ What will you lose if you stay safe, stay here, and don't chase your dreams?

These questions can help you get past perceived limitations and boundaries so that you can go out there and lead like you're meant to! A word of warning: Don't expect to know all the answers on your first try because these aren't questions that have immediate responses. These questions cause you to rethink success in your life and business.

Conclusion

Business owners and leaders need to be good at time management. Instead, many find themselves...

- ➲ Overworked and overwhelmed
- ➲ Struggling with time management
- ➲ Dealing with low confidence
- ➲ Lacking vision

If you spend time putting out fires or managing other people's problems, you won't do the necessary strategic work needed to grow.

Some leaders feel like imposters or like they don't belong. Fortunately, the level to which you feel like an imposter and your level of confidence go hand-in-hand. The imposter feeling fades when you work on your confidence. As a result, other leadership skills will grow stronger.

The reality is that a business owner's vision often dictates the level of business success. By committing to your vision and believing in yourself, you are creating the future of those you lead. You are setting a path now that will determine the legacy you will leave.

It's up to you to stay motivated, take control of your time, commit to your vision, and remain consistent in being the leader you're meant to be.

Chapter 2:

___

A New Leadership Mindset & Framework

Business owners and entrepreneurs often don't have a simple framework to follow to help them overcome and manage the difficulties shared in chapter 1.

The BLUE Shirt Leadership Framework solves these problems and many others. In this book, you will learn to overcome these challenges. But first, we're going to look at the root of these problems and how they're crushing small business owners.

The Starfish

One day, an old man was walking along the beach when he noticed a boy picking something up and gently throwing it into the ocean. He saw the boy doing this over and over as he approached.

Catching up to the boy, the old man asked, "What are you doing?"

The boy replied, "Throwing starfish back into the ocean." The surf was up, and the tide was going out and had stranded hundreds of starfish on the beach. The boy continued, "If I don't throw them back, they'll die."

"Son," the old man said, "don't you realize there are miles and miles of beach and hundreds of starfish? The few you toss back into the ocean won't make a difference."

After listening politely, the boy bent down, picked up another starfish, and threw it back into the surf.

Then, smiling at the old man, he said, "I made a difference to that one."

The BLUE Shirt Leadership Framework unlocks the greatness of your leadership. A BLUE Shirt Leader recognizes that the difference they make starts with one conversation, one employee, one customer, and every interaction they have in a day.

A BLUE Shirt Leader recognizes that the key to leading like they were meant to starts with serving and helping one employee, one friend, and one client at a time.

Unfortunately, the challenges shared in the first chapter that can occur with each new customer, product, or service—along with the many other things a leader is called to do—prevent many leaders from focusing on the most critical work: The important work of developing and growing mindsets, habits, and systems. Many business owners are so busy working in their business that they don't have time to work on themselves, let alone their employees.

Often when a leader tries to do it all on their own, burnout, turnover, and closed businesses are the results. But a leader's work still needs to be done, so how do you keep up?

How Do You Keep Up with It All?

Let's start by looking at the current situation and some interesting facts about small businesses and their owners.

■ Scary Small Businesses Statistics

- ⮐ As of 2020, there were 31.7 million small businesses in the U.S. (99.9 percent of all companies).
- ⮐ Out of the 31.7 million small businesses, 3.7 million are micro businesses, with one to nine employees.
- ⮐ Annually, small businesses create 1.5 million jobs and account for 64 percent of all new jobs in the U.S.

- ⮑ Fifteen million Americans work full-time for their own business.
- ⮑ The number of small businesses in the U.S. has doubled since 1982.
- ⮑ Sixty-six percent of small businesses face financial challenges, with 43 percent stating the most prominent challenge is paying operating expenses.
- ⮑ Eighty-six percent of small businesses would need to supplement funding or cut costs if they lost revenue for two months or more.

Small businesses are the backbone of this country. With so many small businesses making up such a large part of our economy, why are so many business owners struggling to have the balance, consistency, and income they want? Even if you get your MBA, get advice from the SBA, or read business books, most business owners get swept up in the day-to-day work of the business and can't implement even a portion of what they learn about leadership.

How many of these tasks fill your day?

- ☑ Finding customers/clients
- ☑ Wowing customers
- ☑ Marketing and selling
- ☑ Social media engagement
- ☑ Lead generation
- ☑ Hiring talented people
- ☑ Staying productive
- ☑ Financial planning
- ☑ Strategic planning
- ☑ Retaining employees
- ☑ Plus, more!

If all this feels overwhelming, it's because it is. You carry out all these responsibilities in your business day in and day out. Will the BLUE Shirt Leadership Framework make all these go away? No. But you will have a different mindset about these responsibilities and how to handle them better when we are all done.

■ We're Not Complaining

Once upon a time, a wise king constantly heard the same complaints from his people. Being the wise king he was, he decided to tell them a joke, and they all roared with laughter.

After a few minutes, he said he wanted to share another joke with them. So, he told them the same joke, and only a few of them smiled. Then, after the groans stopped, he said the same joke for the third time. This time, no one laughed or smiled.

The king smiled and said, "You can't laugh at the same joke over and over. So why do you always come to me about the same problems?"

Some of you may want to share this story with your employees. But you must agree that we often repeat the same complaints over and over too. If you don't believe me, ask your spouse or a close friend; they'll confirm what I'm saying.

The difficulty may be that you never received the proper training or education to break the cycle. Maybe you missed the training that teaches you how to lead from your strengths, or no one taught you about mindset and habits to avoid and how to discover your best resources for success.

You had the passion and courage to open a business, but that passion and courage can only take you so far. You need the training to help you solve everyday problems. Problems such as marketing, sales, people, and strategy issues don't have immediate solutions, but the BLUE Shirt Leadership Framework will give you the needed help to build a successful business.

■ Small Business Education and Training Failure

A small business owner has an overwhelming amount of work to do. For many small business owners, this overload results in closing their business. The statistics show that one in five businesses close the first year, 49.7 percent by year five, and only 34.5 percent are open after ten years.

Years one through five are the most telling of a business's survival. Regarding training and education on running a small business, 30 percent of owners have no additional education beyond high school. Of those with a college degree, only 9 percent received a bachelor's degree in business. Other surveys show that 54 percent of business owners have had no formal business education.

Small business closures boil down to decisions made by the owner and the mindsets they bring to their business. The buck always stops with the business owner.

According to Guidant Financial, the number one reason people open their business is to be their own boss. The problem is that most people aren't very good at leading themselves, not to mention leading someone else.

Maybe you are just starting, and these statistics and lists feel overwhelming. That's okay. You're not alone. Perhaps you're reading this book and have some success in your business but know there is much more potential. No matter where you are in your business journey, this book provides a framework that will change everything.

Let's look at the old style of leadership and its role in the struggles of today's small business owners.

A Broken Approach to Leadership

Here's some business advice:

In *Star Wars IV: A New Hope*, there's a scene where Admiral Motti wants to start using the Death Star immediately and boldly contradicts Darth Vader's remark that the Death Star's weaponry may not be a match for the Force.

> When someone disagrees with your leadership ideas, never attempt to choke them to death. Darth Vader didn't receive this memo.

Rather than settling the conflict of opinion in a productive, reasonable manner, Vader wastes no time demonstrating his point by using the Force to choke Admiral Motti, just in case the message wasn't clear enough.

Granted, Motti could have shared his suggestion a bit differently, but using force (even if it isn't the mystical one) to resolve disagreements is not the way to go.

Good leaders encourage all voices to be heard and promote open, honest, and inclusive debate. After all, isn't that where the best ideas come from?

You may not see yourself as someone as forceful as Darth Vader, but ponder these questions for a moment:

- ☑ When did you last seek another's perspective, whether it be from someone on your team, a consultant, or a coach?
- ☑ Have you recently cut off someone mid-sentence that was sharing a contradictory idea?
- ☑ Have you avoided someone because they may have feedback you don't want to hear?

In many ways, this leadership style chokes out others from being able to contribute.

Sometimes bad leaders are too stubborn to see their flaws. Other times, they have a self-serving agenda like pursuing power or money, which can be equally damaging to business. Lousy leadership comes in many forms, but the problem always seems rooted in how a leader thinks.

A BLUE Shirt Leader doesn't become easily distracted, sidetracked, or unwilling to adjust. They embrace change and the mental shifts that come with it. Being able to embrace change separates those willing to step up as leaders from those who don't want to shoulder the responsibility.

BLUE Shirt Leaders and business owners must admit their flaws in thinking and behaviors. They recognize the responsibility of leading a business and others.

Embracing change may sound simple enough, but this is no easy task. Distracted and overwhelmed minds are often resistant to change. The fear of taking on something new while trying to manage so much only adds to the resistance. Without change, they are unable to grow. The good news is that you can change your thoughts and create the growth you need.

■ Problems With the Old Leadership Approach

The old approach to leadership focuses on the hierarchy as the structure. The manager or leader is supposed to have more power than subordinates and is the go-to resource for information and decision-making. That was the old-school leadership mindset. Bosses led from the front and were always in charge. That system of thinking does not work in today's business culture.

Traditional leadership has an authoritative tone that leaves little room for people to grow and expand their skill sets. When leaders fall into this approach, it's hard for them to step away from command-and-control behavior.

In traditional organizations, leadership was built around a hierarchical ranking approach. Many leaders that appear judgmental and imposing came from this approach to leadership, resulting in a climate of pessimism and fear among employees.

The old management style hinders building an effective team or organization. Managers get stuck in their heads and don't leave room for others to grow. In this environment, people feel controlled and pressured to work nonstop and remain unmotivated. These approaches pave the way for high turnover rates among staff members and lead many businesses to failure.

An article by The Founder Institute found that of the 600+ companies The Founder Institute helped start, 33 percent are considered high-performing, and 20 percent are considered struggling. The article explains that struggling start-ups have experienced leadership problems ranging from overspending to neglectful behaviors.

Another study by Gallup found that leadership profoundly impacts those they lead. Leadership accounts for 70 percent of the variance in employee engagement. Additionally, only 30 percent of US employees are engaged.

Employee disengagement happens for many reasons, including poor employee relations. It's important to note that employee disengagement is avoidable when you focus on leading well. Did you know:

- The average manager spends over five hours a day on email. (Adobe survey)
- Hiring the wrong person can cost up to 213 percent of their annual salary. (People Keep)
- Companies miss the mark on hiring managerial talent in 82 percent of their hiring decisions.
- The feeling of being undervalued and underappreciated is the number-one barrier to engagement for about 26 percent of employees.

There's clear room for growth, and the command-and-control approach doesn't work. Becoming and staying an effective leader is not something that happens overnight. You need a framework to follow.

The problem is that you must be open-minded as you learn to improve your leadership skills. It takes time and dedication to get there!

Remember, we're looking for progress, not perfection.

Denzel Washington in *The Equalizer*

"I've always done it this way." Too many leaders have said this regardless of the results. Doing something proven to work in the past is a good approach, but as a mantra, failure will be around the corner if you are not open to change.

BLUE Shirt Leadership is about doing something that works and changing as your business environment demands it. If you've been doing things the same way for years and they no longer work, it's time to try something new.

BLUE Shirt Leaders know when to seek advice. Every leader has people around them who want to pull them down or bring them up higher than where they are. As a small business owner, you must constantly look for ways to grow and help others reach their goals. Like the story of the boy with the starfish, it's time to shift your thinking patterns toward one starfish at a time.

■ New Way of Leading

What makes a BLUE Shirt Leader? It's simple, in theory. Build trust, strengthen relationships, and show your employees you believe in them. However, business isn't operated inside a perfect world where all the theories work. Real-world business is a long list of to-dos, putting out fires, and trying to stay sane as you work with vendors, customers, and poorly performing employees while hoping to implement a few new ideas.

The BLUE Shirt Leadership Framework is less about control and more about being focused on creating self-directed teams that can contribute meaningfully.

The opportunity to create a new business environment lies within the creative skill set of your employees, vendors, and virtual assistants. By allowing autonomy, you give them a chance to explore different ways of working or collaborating with others inside and outside their company. By giving those around you freedom with some guidance, you can create an effective business model that benefits everyone involved.

After years of research, powerful mentoring in my life, and testing the framework on dozens of business owners and leaders, the BLUE Shirt Leadership Framework has proven to be an invaluable approach to effective leadership. The framework is anchored by the four pillars mentioned in the metaphor of the Leadership House. Remember that within the BLUE Shirt Leadership Framework, these pillars are:

- **Self-Awareness:** Knowing your limitations and strengths as a leader, understanding the impact your leadership has on others, and also understanding the impact their limitations and strengths have on you.

- **Accountability:** Having a mindset of integrity and following through to help you create a culture of accountability.

- **Growth:** The implementation of ideas and practices to help you grow your leadership and build a team with skills that complement yours.

- **Empowerment:** Giving your team the authority, systems, and resources needed to accomplish what you ask of them.

In the rest of this book, you will learn how to implement this exact framework. The following chapters guide you through each pillar and break them down into the mindsets and behaviors needed to become a BLUE Shirt Leader.

Some of What's to Come

In the **Self-awareness** chapters, you'll discover the myth of self-awareness and how most people aren't in tune with themselves, but BLUE Shirt Leaders are. In chapter 4, you'll learn the five habits of self-aware leaders and how you can implement them into your leadership.

The **Accountability** chapters look at five mindsets that will help you be accountable. These mindsets are what "G.R.I.P.S." the hammer of accountability, described in chapter 6. Chapter 6 also teaches about the Accountability P.A.S.S., a robust process to help you reliably achieve your goals.

Next, you'll dive into the **Growth** chapters. In chapter 7, you'll discover five mindsets, including how maintaining an abundant mindset and persisting as you learn from the risks you take produces significant growth. In chapter 8, you'll develop your vision statement and learn four other habits to help you unlock incredible growth in life and business.

Then, you'll learn what it means to be an **Empowering** leader. Chapter 9 helps unlock your courageous and coaching mindsets and three other key mindsets. Finally, chapter 10 will teach you the five practical habits to empower your team and yourself to be, do, and achieve more.

To wrap up, the last three chapters help you implement everything you have learned, including a chapter on how to implement the BLUE Shirt Leadership Framework in only ten to fifteen minutes a day!

Ready to supercharge your results with the BLUE Shirt Leadership Framework? Don't wait! Apply now for a consultation with Kyle Gillette and receive personalized guidance to fast-track your success. Take the first step towards transformative leadership.

SCAN HERE

Chapter 3:

The Myth of Self-Awareness

■ Awareness

In the early 2000s, I worked in a men's mentoring program called Alpha Academy. Jack Gould, the program's president, was a great leader and had a lot of life and business experience. Jack was an entrepreneur, former California Highway Patrol Officer, deputy sheriff, and a man with great wisdom. His experiences of seeing so many young men caught in street gangs and crime led him to start the Alpha Academy program, which serves eighteen- to twenty-five-year-old men off track in life.

Many of the young men that came to the Alpha Academy program had rough edges. One afternoon, I had a meeting with Jack, a student supervisor named Danny, and one of these students. We had gotten together in the living room of the old farmhouse to speak to the student about his attitude and dedication to the program. The student sat near me on an old striped couch while Jack and Danny sat across the way, with a coffee table between us.

We were about thirty minutes into the meeting, and the conversation had severely escalated. Jack was calmly leading the discussion while trying to keep the student, who was talking, in control, but everything changed in a moment.

The conversation became heated when we asked the student to participate and treat Danny with more respect. Danny responded calmly, but the student started moving toward him, yelling at Danny, and threatening to hurt him. The student was looking for a fight, and Danny was his target.

The student had already been in a fight during his time in the program, consistently threatened violence, and even threatened to harm himself. Jack, the president of the program, stood up slowly and pointed at the student while he walked toward him, saying sternly and calmly, "Get out now. Get out now. Leave. Leave the room. This conversation is over."

Jack was in control of his emotions, and he understood the student's emotions and the gravity of the situation. Every part of his response demonstrated his self-awareness. The student walked out the door within a few seconds of the command, diffusing the situation. Jack controlled himself and was able to bring the problem under control.

Jack exemplifies a leader who has the level of self-awareness of a BLUE Shirt Leader.

■ Most People Aren't Self-Aware

In a study, Tasha Eurich's research team discovered that 95 percent of individuals believe they are self-aware. However, based on a self-assessment procedure, only 10–15 percent were genuinely self-aware.

There are three reasons for this self-awareness disconnect. First, we naturally have blind spots. Second, there is the "feel-good effect": when people see themselves positively, they feel happier. Last, social media has grown exponentially and has negatively impacted self-perception.

Studies have shown that employees are better at recognizing a leader's behavioral tendencies and skill level than the leader is. One survey of over 3,600 leaders in different areas and industries showed that higher-level leaders rated their skills significantly higher than others assessed them.

This pattern existed for nineteen of the twenty competencies the researchers measured, including emotional self-awareness, accurate self-assessment, empathy, trustworthiness, and leadership performance.

In research completed by Chip Heath, David Dunning, and Jerry Suls, studies found that self-assessments of skill and character are often flawed in significant ways and show a low correlation to actual performance.

People's self-view of how well they do something is not always accurate. Sometimes other people know a person better and predict their success better than the person can predict it for him or herself.

The error in self-assessment is pretty evident based on how often people overrate themselves. On average, people say that they are "above average" in skill. How can you have an above-average average?

In the workplace, flawed self-assessment perceptions exist up and down the corporate ladder. Employees overestimate their skills, making it challenging to give meaningful feedback. CEOs also project overconfidence in their judgments, particularly when stepping into new markets or novel projects, making it equally challenging to provide feedback and course correct when needed.

When researchers compare people's self-assessment results of knowledge and skill against their actual performance, there is very little correlation.

■ The Unaware Physical Therapist

A physical therapist coaching client of mine demonstrated this self-awareness gap all too well. After some initial assessments and a few coaching calls, a pattern pointed out how disconnected she was from her behaviors. The following coaching calls focused on team building, time management, and growing the practice.

For the four years before I became her coach, she struggled to keep staff members and move the business forward. According to her, the main reason for the high turnover was that her employees never seemed to be fast enough or smart enough to perform at the level she needed. My job as her coach was to help her to figure out what was "wrong" with the team.

She was a competent physical therapist but not very good at explaining things to her team members. She was highly impatient with their learning processes while labeling some of her employees stupid. In the DISC behavioral patterns, she was a strong D or Dominance (more on this in the section on studying your team).

In one coaching call, I confronted her about her tendency to criticize team members about their performance, but her response was that "no one understood how to do it," followed by, "They are just so slow. They don't understand. I can't train them any more than I already do."

To test my theory of her blind spot in leadership and hopefully help her see it, I observed her and her employees at work for half a day. The team showed low stress, was reasonably efficient, and cared for patients well. But the client's feedback was pessimistic about the team's performance.

After the day wrapped up, I wrote a summary of what I'd seen and spoke to my client about my observations. Ultimately, my client was blind to how her communication style, work pace, and attitude negatively impacted the team, business, and client's perception of their services.

When confronted with this, she could not (or would not) see the connection between the team's performance and her personality and attitude. Two employees had quit within a few weeks of this evaluation, and she was on the hunt again for new employees.

The physical therapist had blind spots. She labeled people stupid and incompetent when they didn't match her personality. She did not want to see herself as the problem, and she tried to replace employees when what she needed to do was adjust her mindset and behaviors.

Her unwillingness to do the mindset work was a missed opportunity, and nothing got through to her despite gentle and direct efforts. After working together for a few months, we parted ways.

■ Internal and External Self-Awareness

Internal self-awareness is the ability to be aware of your feelings and thoughts. It's the ability to be introspective and understand why you feel or think a certain way about a situation. The skill of internal self-awareness can help you better manage your emotions and thoughts, leading to a more productive and happier life.

Internal self-awareness helps you to understand what's happening around you, recognize how you internalize it (even when it seems like people are behaving irrationally), and make better decisions based on your environment.

For example, let's say your team usually meets at 9:00 am, but one day, Joe says he will be late. He ran into some challenges and needed more time than expected.

Would you:

A.   be upset at the delay because you need his presentation ready now, and his delay will get in the way of your workday?

B.   understand that something probably happened that caused the delay, so you're concerned and plan to check in directly with Joe to find out what happened?

C.   immediately think Joe is unreliable and no longer cares to put the work into supporting the team?

If you answered A or C, your internal self-awareness could use some work. Neither of those responses is likely very productive because they aren't reality-based.

Suppose you answered B—congratulations! One of the most significant benefits of self-awareness is that it helps you consider other perspectives and diffuse situations where there isn't much to be upset about.

How To Boost Your Internal Self-Awareness

There are many ways you can boost your internal self-awareness. We will touch on this in chapter 4 when we cover the five habits of self-awareness. For now, journaling and silence (meditation) can go a long way to boost your internal self-awareness.

Journaling is one of the most popular ways to boost your internal self-awareness. It allows you to tap into the deeper parts of your experience and understand why you're feeling or thinking certain things. Journaling helps with self-awareness because it forces you to analyze the thoughts and feelings that are often running through your head and write them out.

Meditation is another excellent way to boost your self-awareness because it helps you clarify what's happening inside. When you're meditating, you're not focused on external stimulation. Instead, you're concentrating on your breathing, thoughts, and emotions by practicing mindful awareness.

In the situation I shared with you about the physical therapist, if the team leader had taken a thirty-second pause to breathe and get her mind settled, and then responded to the situation with much higher self-awareness, she would have been able to see her role differently. I'll offer more on these subjects in the next chapter.

The four pillars of the BLUE Shirt Leadership Framework are essential to focus on daily as a leader. I recommend downloading a digital journal or buying a notebook to help you intentionally reflect on your feelings, habits, and mindsets to create more self-awareness. Next, we will examine external self-awareness and how BLUE Shirt Leaders grow in this area.

How To Have External Self-Awareness

External self-awareness is the ability to see how others perceive you. It's also the ability to understand how your words and actions are impacting other people and how others are impacting your words and actions. Later in this chapter, we will look at several mindsets that will help you gain greater external self-awareness.

- ☑ This awareness can help you manage your relationships and develop better communication skills.
- ☑ For example, let's say you're at a networking event and see someone you know from work. You want to go over and talk to them, but you're unsure if they want to talk to you. They seem to be engaged in a conversation.
- ☑ Would you:
- ☑ go up to them and start talking without knowing if they even want to speak with you?
- ☑ wait for them to come over to you?
- ☑ scan the room for other people you know and see if you can find someone else to talk to?

If you answered A, then your external self-awareness needs some work. People with high external self-awareness would realize that it's best not to invade another person's space by going up and talking to them without an invitation.

Another essential part of your external self-awareness is learning to receive feedback from others. Sometimes that feedback may not be explicit, but by observation in the situation mentioned above, you can interpret the signals.

Receiving feedback also means being open to hearing constructive criticism and accepting what people are saying about you as valid without getting defensive (I'll go more into that in chapter 8).

Here are some tips for increasing your external self-awareness:

1. Pay attention to how you're affecting other people. Pay attention to other people's tones, body language, and the words they choose to use.

2. Be open to direct feedback from others. This type of feedback is when someone speaks directly to you about a situation and what they need from you.

3. Take note of how people are reacting to you. This type of feedback is indirect and unspoken. For example, has the person had an opportunity to make eye contact to get your attention but hasn't? That's feedback. Or maybe when you speak with them, they turn their back on you. That's also feedback.

4. Watch your words and actions carefully. If you pay attention to how others respond to your comments and actions, your external self-awareness will continue to rise.

5. Ask for feedback if something appears unclear. Sometimes you just need to ask people to clarify what they mean when you don't understand something. Asking for clarification can be difficult, but it will resolve many communication problems.

6. Listen carefully when other people speak, and then try to see things from their perspective. As Steven R. Covey says, "Seek first to understand, then be understood."

If you want to become more self-aware in your everyday life, then these are the types of questions you should focus on:

⮕ How do I feel at this moment or about this situation? What do I think about this situation? How can I change my thinking to make it more productive in response to this situation?

⮕ What do others perceive about me, and how am I affecting them? How can I use that information to improve my interactions with others?

⮕ Am I being open enough to feedback from others and accepting what they're saying about me without getting defensive?

⮕ How can I more effectively communicate so that it's clear what I'm trying to say?

⮕ How am I portraying myself through my actions and words? Are those portrayals effective or ineffective?

⮕ How can I change how other people perceive me?

The key to both external and internal self-awareness is being present. As you interact with your team and others, staying in the moment will significantly improve your awareness. The moment you are no longer connected to the moment and start thinking about the next problem or task, your self-awareness suffers.

When you stay present, your team and all those you influence will benefit in those moments, and so will you in the long run. Challenge yourself today to be more present as you lead.

■ Self-Awareness Starts with the Self

Studies show over and over that a lack of self-awareness hurts leaders and those they lead. As seen in the story of the physical therapist and the other examples and statistics mentioned above, most leaders aren't as self-aware as they think.

It is essential to recognize how challenging it is to be and remain self-aware. The good news is that self-awareness is a skill that you can learn and grow. Unfortunately, our level of self-awareness can fluctuate throughout the day and week. We must learn to apply the skill of self-awareness as continuously as possible. By focusing on the following mindsets, you will be better able to achieve a higher level of self-awareness.

Values Mindset

On January 26, 2020, the world lost Kobe Bryant, an icon, alongside eight other people in a horrific helicopter crash. Kobe Bryant was known for his work ethic and phenomenal skills on the basketball court. He was undoubtedly one of the greatest professional basketball players of his generation.

Kobe was truly amazing as a basketball player. He broke numerous records, won five championships, and was a two-time finals MVP, league MVP, and eighteen-time All-Star. But what set him apart was not basketball alone but his ability to remain motivated in any situation and to hold to his values, no matter the cost.

Jay Williams, a former NBA player for the Chicago Bulls, told a story about Kobe Bryant working out before a game. Kobe was already in the gym taking shots and had worked up a serious sweat by the time Jay arrived at the gym.

Jay began his pre-game routine and, after about ninety minutes, stopped his training and sat down, only to see Kobe still practicing. It was another twenty-five minutes before Kobe finally stopped. Jay was amazed at Kobe's work ethic, conditioning, and commitment to the workout.

Jay and Kobe were preparing for the game that night, and despite the intense workout, Kobe scored forty points against the Bulls. After the game, Jay ran up to Kobe to ask him, "Why were you in the gym for so long?" Kobe said, "Because I saw you come in, and I wanted you to know that it doesn't matter how hard you work, that I'm willing to work harder than you."

B.L.U.E Shirt Leadership Framework

The first time I saw Jay tell this story in a YouTube interview, it gave me chills, and I realized there's always room to grow.

In this story, Kobe Bryant exemplified the values of hard work and competitiveness. These values were at the core of who he was on and off the court. Even a cursory search on Kobe Bryant will bring up hundreds of videos and articles of what was dubbed the "Mamba Mentality."

Here's what Kobe said in an interview about this mentality: "Mamba Mentality is all about focusing on the process and trusting in the hard work when it matters most," he said. "It's the ultimate mantra for the competitive spirit. [The Mamba Mentality] started just as a hashtag that came to me one day, and it's grown into something athletes—and even non-athletes—embrace as a mindset."

"Hard work outweighs talent—every time," he added. "Mamba mentality is about 4:00 a.m. workouts, doing more than the next guy, and then trusting in the work you've put in when it's time to perform. Without studying, preparation, and practice, you're leaving the outcome to fate. I don't do fate."

When you lock in your values through a Mamba Mentality, you'll be able to outwork whatever comes your way. Sometimes we need to attack the big bad wolf.

Identifying your values is a worthy endeavor. A great start is to reference the values list at blueshirtcoaching.com/book-resources. Look over the list, find twenty to twenty-five values you identify with, and then narrow down your list to five to seven.

Once you've identified the five to seven values that really matter to you, take a moment to write a definition for each and then place the list where you will see them at work, at home, and on your phone.

The concrete needs rebar when a house foundation is poured to set correctly and not crack. Rebar's primary purpose is to increase the tensile strength of the concrete, helping it resist cracking and breaking. With greater tensile strength, concrete can better resist breaking under tension.

Like rebar, your values help strengthen and reinforce your self-awareness to make decisions that align with who you are as a leader. Your values will help you resist cracking and breaking under the pressures of leadership.

Values will also help you differentiate between the good pressure that helps you to stick to your values and the bad that may break things apart. Your foundation is stronger when you define your values. Strong values result in opportunities for your business and leadership.

Questions To Ponder

Before moving to the next mindset of a self-aware leader, take your notes and respond to the question below.

- ➲ What do you want to shift or reinforce about your values after reading the story about Kobe Bryant?

- ➲ What one value do you know is the rebar needed for your self-awareness foundation?

- ➲ What things, if they were taken away or you couldn't do them, would make your life unbearable? What makes these things valuable to you?

- ➲ Where do you invest the BEST of your time, money, and energy? Why?

Humble Mindset

Humility is not thinking less of yourself. It's thinking of yourself less."

C. S. Lewis.

The goal of a humble mindset isn't to lower your opinion of yourself but to focus on others.

Humility is the opposite of a self-centered attitude. To become a self-aware BLUE Shirt Leader, you need to have humility. The humbler you are, the better your ability to learn from others' feedback.

People with humility can quickly take feedback without getting offended and back up from their failures. Again, humility doesn't mean thinking less of yourself. It means thinking about yourself less often and focusing not on how you look to others but on how you can learn from others.

It's essential to balance humility and pride. It's ok to give yourself time to celebrate your successes. If you're not humble, it's likely that you haven't learned from your mistakes and won't be able to grow as a leader.

The more you can get out of the way of your ego, pride, and self-centered attitude, the better you will perform as a leader. Though we can only see the world through our own eyes, sometimes humility allows us to step back and see it through the eyes of those we lead.

You're probably too hard on yourself and need others to tell you what they see. This humble approach will help you become more self-aware and give you a glimpse of the authentic version of yourself.

Every time you exercise a humble mindset, you serve the people you lead more effectively and glean great insights about yourself and those you lead. Leading from humility also helps in unexpected ways and may have a far more profound impact on people than if you hadn't humbled yourself.

A story about former US Speaker of the House of Representatives Sam Rayburn demonstrates the power of humility and getting out of your own way.

■ Serving Coffee as the Speaker of the House

Sam Rayburn served as Speaker of the House for seventeen years. Through his position he had garnered incredible power and respect. Mr. Rayburn learned that a reporter friend's daughter had tragically died. Mr. Rayburn took it upon himself to go to his friend's home and offer any support.

The reporter didn't believe there was anything he could do since another friend had made all the funeral arrangements. Nevertheless, knowing there is always something a leader can do to serve someone, Representative Rayburn offered to make coffee for the family and simply be there as needed.

Later, Representative Rayburn's reporter friend would recall watching this powerful man make him coffee instead of being at breakfast at the White House with the president. Earlier, Representative Rayburn had sent a message to the president that he had a friend who was in trouble and couldn't make it to breakfast.

Representative Sam Rayburn had a mindset of humility. Despite his great power and obligations, he served his friend in a time of need.

Representative Rayburn through of himself less (by canceling his meeting with the president of the United States) and instead focused on his friend's needs. Suppose you don't have a mindset of humility. In that case, it will be challenging to get outside of yourself and consider the needs of others above yourself in situations like the one Representative Rayburn faced.

The simple way to create more humility as a BLUE Shirt Leader—and, therefore, more external self-awareness—is to begin believing and acting like not everything is about you.

■ Questions To Ponder

➲ How can you show others it isn't all about you?

➲ Who needs to see a humbler version of you?

➲ Who can you reach out to help keep you on track regarding remaining humble?

Knowing your values and staying aware of what may hinder genuine humility in your leadership requires internal and external focus. The BLUE Shirt Leadership Mindset works through building self-reflective practices and consistently applying them. This process requires patience, but it pays off in the long run.

Patience Mindset

Understanding the growth of a bamboo tree can serve as a metaphor for patience. It takes five years for a Chinese bamboo tree to begin to grow. When you place a bamboo seed in the ground, you must water the seed every day for five years before the first bamboo shoot can be seen.

Once the bamboo finally shoots through the soil, it can grow to ninety feet tall in just five weeks. But none of this will occur if the seedling is not continuously watered and fertilized.

As a BLUE Shirt Leader, you must be patient like a gardener nurturing a bamboo seedling. Sometimes there may appear to be minimal results from your professional development efforts, but these practices pay off over time. Like the bamboo tree, your patience will blossom into new self-awareness and growth in your BLUE Shirt Leadership journey in time.

You can continue this cycle, build self-awareness, and grow as a leader. To develop your businesses and leadership, you must be patient as you read, write, and act. The patience mindset is like the role of an architect in designing a home.

An architect works on the smallest details, catches the tiniest errors in design, and designs a stable and beautiful structure. The more patient you are with the process, the stronger and more intricate your leadership house can be.

It takes time to build a great home, and it takes time to become a BLUE Shirt Leader. BLUE Shirt Leaders recognize the importance of patience with themselves, their team, and their business. Patience allows you to be the architect of your leadership house.

The idea is simple: *Slow down to leadership up.*

■ Areas Where Patience Is Vital

Being patient with yourself is a great place to start. You don't know everything, and there is always room to grow as a leader. Be patient as you learn your strengths and limitations. As mentioned at the beginning of this book, becoming a BLUE Shirt Leader is about working hard on your strengths and helping others to do the same.

Don't waste time focusing on your weaknesses, but instead manage them and surround yourself with people that have strengths in the areas of your weaknesses. Teams designed to support each other's weaknesses produce far greater results than teams full of individuals trying to be good at everything.

BLUE Shirt Leaders are patient with themselves and understand that they can reach their potential and help their team members do the same. Instead of focusing on their weaknesses, BLUE Shirt Leaders learn to manage them.

Be patient with your team. Your team members are going through their own growth and development processes. Figure out what their strengths are and help them build on those strengths. Also, take time to make a synergistic team that brings all the strengths together and, as a result, overcomes any individual limitations.

The mindsets in chapters 5 and 9 will give you insights on how to help you trust the systems, set goals, get priorities dialed in, and collaborate with your team.

Be patient with the sales and marketing parts of your business. My marketing and networking efforts have sometimes paid off in thousands of dollars within days. However, most of the time, achieving success takes much longer. I recently had a client hire me after two years of marketing and connection with her.

Most businesses grow like bamboo trees. Slow growth is a good thing. Over time, you will have the sales and marketing foundation to withstand whatever the big bad wolf throws your way. Letting your social media, networking, and marketing get rooted well will give you a firm business foundation. Notice the mindsets and habits that lead to your success during the slow-growth period. It will pay off. Be patient with this process.

Be patient with your customers/clients. Sometimes customers are wrong, pains in the backside, and frustrating. Your customers are humans too. Set clear expectations with customers and how your team interacts with them. Being patient with customers can be as simple as listening to their complaints and serving the need(s) you discover.

Sometimes clients won't even meet you halfway. Sometimes they fail at following through on what they say they will do. If you've ever spoken to an accountant before, I'm sure you've heard them comment about clients waiting until the last minute to give them the documents they needed.

Whatever the case may be, your patience will pay off—maybe not with the specific customer or client you're thinking of right now, but at some point in the future.

■ Think, Feel, Choose

Galatians 5:22–23 (NLT) reads, "But the Holy Spirit produces this kind of fruit in our lives: love, joy, peace, patience, kindness, goodness, faithfulness, gentleness, and self-control. There is no law against these things!" The word "patience" is not about the ability to wait but how we act while waiting. The "think, feel, choose" mantra is an effective way to choose how to act as a BLUE Shirt Leader while waiting.

When clients cancel or fail to follow through on their commitments, the "think-feel-choose" mantra creates space to be patient with them. When my daughters or wife frustrate me about something, the "think-feel-choose" mantra creates space to be patient with them.

Dr. Caroline Leaf, author of Switch on Your Brain, teaches this mantra to help us slow down and get our thoughts under control. I want to share with you how this served me as a leader. When a client texted asking if we could switch our coaching session to a different day, I took a moment and repeated "think-feel-choose" several times.

I wanted to text, "Why are you changing this appointment? Were you not able to follow through on your commitments? I'm not sure I can honor a shift in the schedule."

Instead, I texted, "What's the reason for the change?" Over the weekend, an employee had died of cancer, and he needed time to grieve and think.

Imagine his response and my horror had I not slowed down a bit, been patient with myself and him, and taken time to "think-feel-choose."

When you begin to feel, and your emotional energy goes where you don't want it to, repeat to yourself the phrase "think-feel-choose." Start by saying think, then say feel and follow this with an extended *chooooose*.

Repeat this phrase several times. Then address the situation. The beauty of using this as a tool to control yourself and build patience is that it takes only three to five seconds and will reset your mind and pace.

Try it now. You'll notice the difference.

■ Questions To Help You Be More Patient

⮑ If you could do today (this week) all over again, what would you do differently?

⮑ What was your predominant attitude today (this week)?

⮑ How do you think others perceived you today (this week)?

Record your answers in your notes before you move on to the next mindset.

Trusting Mindset

Several months ago, I had a call with my coach. We were talking about trusting myself and my processes. During that call, I realized my trust level in these areas was significantly higher than ever, but there were still other areas of struggle.

My coach began to unravel the reality that there was a lack of trust in myself, and I saw where I was overextending myself.

As we continued the coaching call, she pushed. During that call, I realized I needed to trust people to do what they are great at and trust the systems we use.

As business owners, we tend to overextend ourselves in our weak areas. We try to be all things to all people. We try to be superheroes. As a result, we become too controlling people and things. Results are not optimal when trust is low.

When you doubt others or yourself, you do things that don't fit your strengths or fall in alignment with your values, and you micromanage and limit what's possible. The reality? You can't do it all and will feel overwhelmed by everything there is to do.

But if you trust your strengths and the strengths of others, it will make a tremendous difference in your results.

■ Island-Hopping

Shortly after this conversation with my coach, I took an island-hopping flight with my wife. We started from a tiny little airport strip in our neighborhood to an island about thirty minutes away. We trusted our pilot to get us from our home to the island and back safely. It ended up being a fantastic date.

When you trust the skills of others and your instincts in your business, you will experience significant results and be able to do things you could never have before.

While sitting in that sixty-year-old Cessna 182 and waiting for the pilot to run through the checklist squished next to my wife, I was nervous, but I had trust. You, too, might be worried about letting someone else pilot a project or situation, but you still can set your mind to trust them. I knew the pilot had over twenty years of experience, and I didn't. It's probably wise for me to trust him to do what he's best at instead of trying to take over.

There are people on your team, consultants, and business partners out there waiting for you to allow them to be the pilot on a project. They are the ones that YOU are making nervous because you are trying to fly the plane when they are the skilled pilots! Our goal that afternoon was to go to the island. The pilot's goal was to fly us there safely. Everyone wins by trusting each other with what we are skilled to do.

Trust will be easy to give when you can communicate your priorities and goals and develop proper systems. If you struggle with trusting your employees (or vendors, contract labor, etc.), the chapters on empowerment (chapters 9 and 10) will help you immensely with this.

It's okay to admit you don't know everything. Once you realize this and begin to trust what you've created and whom you work with, you will notice more and more areas where trusting others is the smart move. Too many business owners try to be pilots in situations that are really out of their league.

What would have happened if I had taken over and tried to fly the plane? Know your strengths and your team's strengths, and everyone will soar!

Don't be the business owner who does everything and ends up crashing.

Tools like the DISC personality profile assessment will help to reveal a lot about how a team can best work together or how you can best work with a coach/consultant. People love to learn about themselves. The DISC assessment helps assessment-takers and their leaders better understand communication patterns and tendencies. When you gain more clarity around how someone does something and why, your level of trust in them increases significantly.

You'll learn about DISC in more detail in chapter 10.

■ Four Ways To Build Trust

As mentioned in chapter 2, the old leadership style doesn't work anymore. When building trust with your team, embracing the new leadership style is essential. BLUE Shirt Leadership is about inspiring, supporting, serving, shifting your leadership, and building trust. To build that trust, you must:

1. Pay attention to your track record and that of your employees. Take a moment to review the success of each employee and give them the respect they deserve for their achievements and progress. It's easy to miss the growth if you're overwhelmed and doing too much.

2. A trusting mindset is an open mindset. Be the example when you fail. Be the example when you succeed. Vulnerability and transparency build a trusting environment.

3. As a BLUE Shirt Leader, create a culture that invites open communication through your example. With this comes the need to provide the necessary time, resources, and tools for open communication.

4. Finally, be courageous. Sometimes you don't know what to do. You should be willing to share this. Be bold in trusting your team. Be brave in trusting your instincts. When you have courage, you will show humility as never before. When you do this, you teach your team to be courageous.

■ Questions To Help You Build a Trusting Mindset

- ➲ What skills and systems do you have that you can trust?
- ➲ What are the top strengths of your team members or consultants?
- ➲ What can you do to allow others to leverage their strengths inside and outside your organization to bring it more success?

Observant Mindset

As I get older, I pay less attention to what people say and more attention to what they do."

Andrew Carnegie

I met with a lady at a coffee shop for a networking conversation. I'd seen her on stage before presenting and briefly chatted with her at networking events, but we'd never had a formal introduction or an extended discussion.

While standing in line for coffee, I noticed (despite the mask) that she was smiling and had a positive attitude. I knew we were going to have a lively conversation. I also knew I needed to give her space to share and ask questions that would draw from her what was important to her for this meeting.

After settling into our seats and exchanging a few words, I asked her what got her interested in her field. After a few minutes of chatting, she mentioned something about her strengths. So, I followed up with a question about what she knew about her strengths.

After a while, we talked about European history, one of her passions. This discussion led to other historical topics, including business, local and international history, etc. At one point, she mentioned investing. When there was a lull in the conversation, I brought this up, and off we both went to talk about the market and real estate investing.

The conversation flowed like this for ninety minutes. It was a great experience. While I was observant to catch the nuances of her interests, she was also great at doing the same for me.

It's conversations like these that lead to many things—in her case, a guest appearance on my podcast and who knows what for our further networking. Either way, enjoyable and productive conversations result when you maintain an observant mindset. This conversation was no exception!

Here's the catch: I'm not nearly as interested in history as she is, and real estate investments are intriguing but not my focus right now. But because I was working to have an observant mindset, I thoroughly enjoyed the conversation and learned a lot in the process.

BLUE Shirt Leaders have learned to work hard at tuning into the people they are speaking to, listening to, or coaching. They have this uncanny ability to spot a nuance in communication that allows them to connect at a deeper level with the other person.

These leaders tune into the four communication channels, listening much more deeply than most other people.

■ The Four Channels of Communication

First, BLUE Shirt Leaders are adept at the three v's of communication. We've all heard of these communication channels before. They are verbal, vocal, and visual. The verbal channel is the words we speak. This channel makes up 7 percent of the *meaning* of our communication.

The next channel is vocal. This channel is the intonation in our voice. The vocal makes up 38 percent of the *meaning* in our communication. Then, we have visual or body language. Body language makes up the remaining 55 meaning of the *meaning* of our communication.

Many leaders are aware of the fourth channel of communication but don't spend much time focusing on developing this channel. Often, I hear leaders speak of using this channel of communication when they hire someone. They'll say, "I just knew she was the right one." "I had a feeling he would work out." "My gut told me not to hire him."

The fourth channel of communication that a BLUE Shirt Leader uses to observe others is intuition. Intuition is the channel of communication based on your gut feelings and experience. When you are tuned in to your intuition, you are open to using this as a tool for self-awareness. Intuition comes from your unconscious, the part of your mind that is always recording and storing your memories and taking in all that your senses give it.

At times, our unconscious will alert us to something, and then our conscious becomes aware of a "feeling" or "sense" we need to explore further. A more technical definition of intuition is "arriving without inference or using reason." Some have said it is a type of "direct knowing."

An example of intuition as a type of direct knowing is when you ask the perfect question that draws out needed insight. We will look at intuition in detail in the next chapter.

As you think about these four communication channels, ask yourself the following questions:

- What emotions did you experience from other people today? How did those emotions impact you?
- What did you notice about the visual and vocal communication you heard today?
- What did your intuition communicate to you today? Did you act on it?
- How did you treat others the way they wanted to be treated?
- What was something someone said you could follow up on just to connect more deeply with them?

■ Conclusion

To wrap up this chapter, and before moving on, take the time to review the questions presented to help you become a better leader, and then take some notes on your responses. Ultimately, great self-awareness in your BLUE Shirt Leadership begins with having the right mindsets. When you purposefully work on the five mindsets in this chapter, you'll find new levels of self-awareness in your life and your business.

To apply these mindsets to your leadership, start with defining your values and allowing the pressure the world exerts on those values to help you become more self-aware and a better leader. As you grow in your leadership, remain in a humble mindset by thinking of yourself less and focusing on others.

With this higher level of awareness, you will surely bump into moments of impatience with yourself and others. Remember to ask yourself the right questions in those moments and to take a moment to breathe or write. As these mindsets build, you will trust yourself and your team more while becoming a master observer of people.

In the next chapter, you'll learn the practical ways to apply these mindsets to your everyday business experiences.

Chapter 4

The Habits of Self-Aware Leaders

Self-awareness means understanding that communication is bi-directional. What and how you say something is just as important as how you listen and process what others say. You also need to understand that everyone communicates differently. As you learned in the previous chapter, communication is a skill that all leaders need to practice and develop.

We communicate all the time using the four forms of communication. Becoming a great communicator is an ongoing quest to tune into the four channels of communication–verbal (words), vocal (tone), visual (body language), and intuition.

Being highly observant and skilled in these four channels is why BLUE Shirt Leaders are excellent communicators. BLUE Shirt Leaders' observations within these channels assist them in leading their teams to a successful future.

The BLUE Shirt Leadership Framework helps us use these observations and change our mindsets, emotions, and behaviors. These observations significantly impact our leadership success or failure, and they are all connected.

The Platinum Habit

Dr. Tony Alessandra is the founder of Assessments 24x7, which has provided hundreds of thousands of assessments to people worldwide. He and his team have helped thousands learn a new way to communicate with those they lead. He says we need to "treat others the way they want to be treated." This is a departure from the "Golden Rule," which says, "Treat people how you want to be treated."

This shift toward the "Platinum Habit" is the communication approach BLUE Shirt Leaders use.

BLUE Shirt Leaders recognize that everyone has a different world map and work to better understand what the map of those they lead looks like. The Platinum Habit helps you remain observant of others' world maps and then adjust your communication to fit theirs.

■ Find the Twenty Percent

The Platinum Habit seems a strange fit for self-awareness, but as you take the time to observe other people and stay curious about those you lead, you'll notice there are minor shifts you can make in your leadership. The big bad wolf wants you to stay where you are as a leader. He wants you to get comfortable with your style and to believe that people need to adjust to you. After all, you're the leader. It's their job to learn to listen to you.

However, the BLUE Shirt Leader doesn't remain static in their leadership and how they lead others. The BLUE Shirt Leader takes time to look and learn how the people they lead differ from themselves. In this process, they become more aware of others, their needs, communication styles, and themselves.

Yes, it's easier to lead as you always do, but when you lead as you always do, you will get the results you always get. And yes, it's difficult to treat people the way they want to be treated, but when you do, you're becoming a BLUE Shirt Leader.

The Platinum Habit is a guide on how to develop your communication skills so that you can best serve others. Another tool for helping develop communication skills is DISC. DISC is a personal development assessment tool that breaks down communication styles into four groups.

I'll give you an example of how understanding someone's communication style contributed to one client's success. Sally is the event director of a major resort. I began her coaching by looking at her DISC assessment results and discussing the Platinum Rule and how we would use both as a base for how she communicated with others.

In one session, Sally announced she had some fantastic news she wanted to share. It seems a senior member of Google reached out to her, and they were searching for locations to hold an event at the end of the year.

As she continued her story, she became more and more animated. What she was excited about was that the more she talked to the Google representative, the better she could tune into his DISC communication profile and redirect her communication style with him.

By utilizing the Platinum Habit and what she knew about communication styles based on DISC, she wrote a proposal to suit him rather than sending a one-size-fits-all message. She eventually won the $500,000 contract, and he later thanked her for how she communicated with him during the process.

Two things happened here: 1) Sally found the difference between her communication and his; and 2) she was self-aware enough to know her communication style and be able to adjust it to fit him.

■ Four Actions To Help You with the Platinum Habit

1. Slow down or speed up your communication by using the four communication channels— verbal, vocal, visual, and intuition—to better connect with clients, prospects, and employees.

2. Ask yourself the following question to determine if you should slow down or speed up: *Is this person speaking at a faster or slower pace than I am?* Make your adjustment to their speed, regardless of whether your pace is normally fast or slow.

3. Listen more and talk less. If you adjust even slightly and allow the other person more time to speak, you will shift the pattern. The shift will be worth it. I talk more about this in the empowering mindsets chapter.

4. Don't assume; ask. Ask people what their preferred method of communication is. Do they prefer text, email, phone, or in-person information and updates? This simple question will pay dividends for your bottom line.

■ Questions To Ponder

- ➲ Who can you apply the Platinum Habit to?
- ➲ Who on your team or in your network may benefit from a better understanding of this habit?
- ➲ What one shift in focus can you make today to put this habit into practice?

The Intuitive Habit

My awareness of my gifts regarding interpersonal relationships was just beginning to show when I first developed the BLUE Shirt Leadership Framework. Soon after starting my business, this awareness would grow tremendously.

After leaving my job in human resources and working within my natural skill set, it was as though a curtain was being opened. I could not only think for myself but also act without getting trapped in the chain of command that the corporate structure creates.

The new freedom of life and mind allowed me to learn at a greater rate and whatever I wanted. My mind was opened to a new level of awareness and ability. This mind and life freedom drove me to achieve and pursue big things more confidently than ever before.

The freedom also brought new awareness to my life and business skills. To be sure, there were nerves and concerns about whether I'd be able to hack it in the coaching and consulting world. But through experiences and a few key conversations, those concerns quickly faded.

One of those conversations was with Steve Sisler. He is known as an intuitive savant. During a consulting call, he reviewed some of my assessment results and made two comments that I still think about.

The first comment was about my success trajectory.

Steve first told me on that call, "Kyle, from your profile, I'm sensing that you will take off and find success after you turn forty."

We will see what happens with this one. Things are going well now, and I'll hit forty in 2023. Stay tuned!

Next, he pointed out that my approach to speaking and workshops should change. The conversation went like this.

Steve: "Do you do workshops or presentations?"

Me: "I just started doing this."

Steve: "Do you follow a script or prepare for these presentations?"

Me: "Yes, a lot."

Steve: "You will do much better if you don't prepare as much and trust yourself and your intuition more."

Based on the two assessments he did and his feedback, something clicked. This conversation was a critical self-awareness moment. This new nugget of knowledge unlocked my confidence and thousands of dollars of new and repeated revenue for my business.

Before this call, I had spent so much time trying to perfect my knowledge and have all the answers, only to appear disingenuous and disconnected from my clients. I knew it, and so did the people I was presenting to. I was afraid to change and embrace who I really am.

When you know yourself intimately, your confidence shifts in profound ways, if you remember from the first chapter, low confidence hinders your success as a leader and, therefore, your business success. The Platinum Habit and the next four habits will change this and much more. The next essential self-awareness habit is trusting your intuition.

A powerful part of self-awareness is to learn to go with your gut or intuition. But sometimes, it's hard to know if it's intuition or simply a guess. I want to teach you how to decipher the difference and become more in tune with yourself.

■ $50,000 Intuition Payoff

During my first coaching conversation with Chuck, we talked about him developing a marketing program for one of his business clients in the construction industry. But when I followed up, he hadn't taken any steps forward.

During the conversation I asked him if he thought the marketing program would work and be effective or if he had any doubts. His response was straightforward. He knew it would work. I wanted to know how he knew.

Our intuition is the ability to "know" something at a deeper level than knowing something based on facts. Most of us need to tune into this "knowing" to understand the difference between knowing on an intuitive level and guessing.

As you may remember, intuition is the fourth communication channel. It comes from external, internal, and experiential angles. Sometimes we have all the facts, we have thought about the details, and everything lines up, so we go for it. We've done the same level of due diligence but lack all the answers and somehow still go for it.

When working with Chuck, he "knew" this proposed marketing program would work and that he could scale it. He lacked detailed proof that it would work, but something in his gut told him to go for it nonetheless. When he did, the prospect immediately loved the plan, resulting in a $50,000 contract. That's not all. He's written two more contracts for the same program since.

No one else was doing what he was proposing, but he knew in his gut it was the path to pursue. He has made over six figures in just a few months by learning to trust his intuition.

From my experience, intuition comes as "a thought that is not my own." I believe God's prodding of my unconscious provides the sense of knowing that allows me to make that leap into the intuitive realm. It may be different for you. In any case, it comes from a unconscious place along with internal and external sources.

■ What Is Intuition?

Intuition is a form of unconscious knowledge. Yet, it's not just your knowledge but all the information and experiences you hold in memory and unconscious observation (see chapter 3). Without us even being aware, the brain sorts and files all types of information, just waiting for it to be retrieved at the right time. Your intuition works in some ways as the processor of all that unconscious stuff to help make sense of what you already know.

Have you ever felt that something is the right thing to do and then done it? When we tap into our intuition, our brain has made a unconscious decision without us knowing all that went into the choice. BLUE Shirt Leaders are adept at using their intuition as a decision-making tool.

The more you think of your decision-making process as intuitively based vs. strictly logical, the easier it becomes to make better decisions.

Intuition is also great for recognizing when something just doesn't feel right. If you get an inner gut feeling about a person, place, or thing that makes you cautious, it can indicate something isn't quite right. It could mean that you may have forgotten something, or something is not quite right about the person or situation.

Intuition develops from your experiences, observations, reflective times, and empirical knowledge. Your intuition may help you ask insightful questions, make judgments, or identify when something is amiss, But only if you listen to it.

Learning to listen to your intuition is like any other skill—it takes practice, patience, and consistent effort. Developing the ability to trust your intuition leads you down the path of becoming a great leader.

You might think, "I'm just not intuitive." The truth is that we all possess intuition; it's a brain function. Some people have a greater awareness of it than others, but everyone has some degree of intuition in them.

Business owners can benefit from using their intuition when making business decisions. It can be as simple as deciding something feels off or is not quite right. Stop and try to figure out what is holding you back. Your intuition will tell you when it is safe to move forward.

Great leaders tap into their intuition all the time. They regularly trust themselves to make decisions based on their gut feelings as a guide. Take the time to reflect on a recent decision that may have felt more intuitive than logic based, and then note your answers to the following questions in your journal:

- What were the circumstances? (day/night, location, time, emotions)
- How did you "know" your choice was the right choice?
- Where did you "feel" this intuition coming from?
- How can you replicate this sort of experience?

When people share stories, an exciting communication phenomenon can be observed on MRI brain scans. Whether the story is sad, exciting, scary, or in any other genre, the listener's brain scan reveals that all the same brain areas are lighting up or showing activity as the storyteller's brain. They are sharing the experience on a biochemical level.

BLUE Shirt Leaders' intuition operates like this. In addition to noticing patterns in situations and things, BLUE Shirt Leaders unconsciously tune into other people's brain patterns, trust this information, and allow it to impact their decision-making. Their unconscious then brings this to their attention, and the leader follows their intuition.

Let's look at how you can shape this habit and skill too. You can tune into your intuition by being mindful of your thoughts and feelings when listening to what others say about you. You'll wonder, "Why am I feeling this way?" or "Should I do what I'm thinking about?"

When you experience a sense of knowing what to do next without knowing why, or that walking away from a conversation (or saying something) is just not right, these are intuitive moments. Pause and reflect on where the specific "thought that's not your own" comes from.

Does the feeling or thought come from your stomach, heart, outside your head, etc.? For me, intuition seems to flow around my head and manifest as a new insight. If you can figure out how intuition "arrives" in your mind and body, then it is much easier to trust the insights when they show up.

If that's too far-out for you, here are two other simple actions you can take to tune into intuitive leadership. First, go for an "intuitive walk" where you listen to your thought patterns, listen for specific words, and take the time to observe others and your environment. What you are drawn to will tell you more than you might know.

Alternatively, simply follow your enthusiasm to where it is taking you. When we are excited, that feeling often comes from a place of being in alignment—that alignment of thought, gut, and heart.

Writing is an intuitive tool as well. If you didn't do the writing exercise above, take the time to do it now before you read this next section.

The Writing Habit

According to a study by *Psychology Today*, 50 percent of people have used a journal sometime in their life, and 16 percent are currently using a journal. The research shows that many people see the benefits of maintaining a writing habit. Those benefits include:

- Reduced stress
- Improved immune function
- Improved memory
- Elevated mood
- Healthier emotional responses

I don't remember who first suggested that I journal, but I'm glad they did. I jumped on the journaling train when I was sixteen years old and have been on it almost every day since.

The entries are now less about girls and basketball, the daily thoughts of a sixteen-year-old boy, and more about an adult's meaningful business and life challenges. There have been nuggets of new awareness, intuitive insights, and confidence-building opportunities recorded through it all. All this journaling has led me toward more self-awareness, peace, and progress.

If you haven't journaled before, now is a great time to start. If you have in the past dropped off, please get back to it. In some ways, you have already begun journaling if you jotted down your answers to the questions asked along the way.

In the business world, journaling sounds strange, but why resist writing your thoughts on paper or digitally to help clear your mind and find insights, patterns, and opportunities that you may not have seen before just because some might think it strange?

I began doing digital journals in 2014, and it is a fascinating journey of reflection to pick a random date in my journal and see what I was working on. What I read often becomes an encouragement when I see my progress in life and business.

Here are three writing methods to help you become more self-aware and grow yourself and your business.

■ Three Journaling Methods

Get a pen and notebook and write

Write at least one sentence per day, every day. You can answer a couple of questions to help you be more reflective or write whatever is on your mind. The key is the habit of at least one sentence per day, every day. A great way to start any journal entry is to include one to three things you are grateful for. If you do just that, what you write will positively impact you.

Start with Gratitude

Sometimes the best starting point is to begin your day by writing down the five things you are grateful for. These can be as simple as the carpet under your feet, a good night of sleep, your spouse, or the color blue! The goal is to create a positive and abundant attitude to start your day..

Do NeuroCycle journaling

Neurocycling is a method developed by Dr. Caroline Leaf that helps you center yourself and write your thoughts in a way that looks more like a mind map. This approach reflects your thought patterns in your mind like a tree rather than in a linear, long-form written format.

This method is specifically helpful for eliminating toxic thoughts and, therefore, behaviors. This works by putting the toxic thought in the center of a page, then drawing lines outward to the five categories of origin story, emotional warning signals, physical warning signals, perspective, and behaviors. You then build a linking web from each category and slowly add to it over consecutive days.

The goal is to find the journaling approach that best fits you. Each of these approaches can take between five and twenty-five minutes per day, depending on how much you have to say!

The Silence Habit

In the busyness of business, silence is a luxury that few of us experience daily.

Fortunately, the absence of silence is something you can change. For small business owners and leaders, finding the time to do this can be challenging, but it is possible. This chapter will look at three methods to create more silence in your life and leadership. The goal of practicing the habit of silence is to help you be present.

As a leader, it's easy for you to get lost in the day's problems or the next month's issues or tune out altogether. The habit of silence helps you to stay in the here and now and focus your energy on the conversation you're in, the meeting you need to prep for, or the sales call you must close.

Here's what won't work for 90 percent of us when it comes to silence:

- ⮥ One-hour meditation and silence in the morning
- ⮥ Yoga and monthly meditation retreats
- ⮥ Silent walks in the middle of the workday

While these habits are all very effective and worth striving for, most of us probably can't fit any of them into our schedules. But we can be purposeful to transition well from one role or activity to the next.

■ Transition Moments

I want you to imagine for a moment that your computer's browser windows and tabs represent your leadership. The windows represent your roles, and the tabs are the activities of those roles. Often, leaders forget to close the windows and tabs as they transition from role to role.

Throughout your day, you can quickly review what's going on in your browser window (role) and tabs (tasks), then close them down before you move to the next window and tabs. Every window and open tab uses a computer's processing power. It is the same for your leadership.

When you practice the habit of silence, you give yourself the space to bookmark your tabs and close windows, providing energy to the new window and tabs. If you don't, your leadership energy is drained, and your ability to be present and focused on the current role and tasks suffers significantly.

I suggest you use transition moments to open and close the right window. Every day you go through dozens of transitions (or role changes). After writing this section, I'll transition out of my writing window (role) and into a networking call. There is an opportunity for me to take a few seconds to transition well here. I could leave the writing "window" open in my leadership browser and then open the networking window. But that leaves an energy drain on my focus.

Instead of leaving both windows open, I'll take ten to sixty seconds to practice silence and make sure I can close one window before I open the other. This habit requires me to be much more present and in tune with what I've accomplished in that role before moving onto the next role.

In this example, just after I finish the last sentence of my writing, I will breathe for ten to sixty seconds to become fully present and determine what I need to do to close that leadership window. In the following few paragraphs, I'll explain what to do during these ten- to sixty-second transition periods to get the most out of them.

These transition opportunities allow you to turn your focus 100 percent to the right window and close the other windows that are draining your energy. Like computers, we can trust that the next time we open that browser window, the tabs and information will still be there.

Transitions are opportunities to ground yourself and stay present. Below is a list of some everyday transition moments in your workday.

- When switching from a conversation with an employee to a call with a customer
- When you get back from having coffee or lunch with a friend
- Just before you get out of your car to head into your home
- Before a sales call you have to make
- Before you begin an interview with a potential employee
- When someone interrupts your workflow
- After a tense conversation

Each of these situations (and many more) requires you to switch from one role to another. As you recognize these transitions, you can choose to do one of two things. You can be silent and observant, or you can choose to leave both windows (or more) open and let them drain your energy.

Silence is about quieting your thoughts and slowing your momentum so you can listen. The following method will help you do this more effectively in the middle of a busy workday.

The next time you switch from being the boss to walking into your home, take three long breaths to quiet your thoughts and slow your movements. After the breaths, take ten to sixty seconds to bookmark those tabs on your boss browser window and close it down. Then purposefully open the parent or significant-other window before you get out of the car.

As you do this, an idea pops into your mind. You recall a task you need to complete. An email reply comes to mind, or some other type of distraction pulls you out of the silence. That's okay. Let the idea pass through your mind. Trust it will come back to you.

Continue to stay in the moment and allow your mind to be quiet. Stay in tune with your breathing. After a few breaths and moments of reflection, close the tabs and window on the previous role. Once you've done this, you can open the new window and think about what tabs need to be open as you walk into your home in your new role.

These ten- to sixty-second transition moments result in more energy toward the new role, more awareness, and more peace, too. These brief moments of silence are like reset buttons for your mind and heart.

Don't be surprised if you notice more things after you get into this habit of silence. With more energy to give the new role, some new observations will come your way, such as:

- ☑ Non-conversational sounds you didn't notice before
- ☑ More awareness of what activities people are engaging in
- ☑ Minor changes to the environment
- ☑ More awareness of the emotions of others
- ☑ The three V's stand out much more clearly
- ☑ You become a better listener
- ☑ And much more

Ultimately, the habit of silence helps you become more grounded in yourself. When you use intentional breathing, you allow yourself to become more self-aware of your thoughts, feelings, and presence. Slowing down and breathing allows you to process what your mind is working on. You will also be less stressed, more aware, and a better leader when you do this.

These short moments of silence are what BLUE Shirt Leaders use to stay entirely engaged in the many roles they fill throughout the day. BLUE Shirt Leaders also take the time to practice the habit of silence as part of their morning or evening meditation practices. In the next section, I'll teach you about a specific meditative approach and how you can use this meditative practice to bring more silence into your life.

■ The BOTES Meditation Method

Meditation helps you step through the four pillars of BLUE Shirt Leadership. This practice will help you become more self-aware, remind you of the things you need to be accountable for, and help you maintain a growth mindset. Finally, practicing meditation engages your mind on what you can do to empower others.

A simple way to prepare yourself to practice the habit of silence is to use a simple breathing practice. Find a comfortable position to sit, either on the floor or in a comfortable chair. Next, close your eyes and breathe in for five seconds through your nose, hold for a count of five, and then blow out for five seconds. Repeat this three to five times to prepare for your meditation practice.

After you've completed your breaths to quiet your mind and body, you'll let your mind "float in BOTES" by reflecting on five areas: Body, Others, Thoughts, Emotions, and Spiritual self. Spend three to five minutes focused on each area, using the four BLUE Shirt Leadership Framework pillars—self-awareness, accountability, growth, and empowerment—to guide your focus. The following questions are only suggestions. You can simply think about the four pillars for a few minutes and trust your mind to guide you where you need to go.

Self-awareness: Meditate on your whole being

- ➲ *Body*: What am I feeling in my body? Start at your toes and work to the top of your head.
- ➲ *Others*: What awareness do I have about my impact on others, good or bad?
- ➲ *Thoughts*: What mindsets and beliefs am I experiencing?
- ➲ *Emotions*: What emotions am I currently experiencing?
- ➲ *Spiritual self*: What is happening in my life spiritually?

Accountability: Meditate on your promises

- ⮂ What promises have I made about taking care of my physical body?
- ⮂ What promises have I made to others that I need to keep? Think about the people in your life that you influence.
- ⮂ In what ways do I need to be more accountable in my thought life? Are negative thoughts, doubts, or worries creeping in?
- ⮂ What is coming up emotionally that I need to be accountable for? How are my emotions not where they need to be?
- ⮂ What sort of spiritual accountability would be helpful for me right now?

Growth: Meditate on your development

- ⮂ In what ways am I improving myself physically? What needs to change?
- ⮂ How am I helping others grow? Who is coming to mind that I could help?
- ⮂ Where do I have a fixed or scarcity mindset? In what areas of life do I need to have an abundance mindset? Think about your relationships, thought patterns, or areas of fear.
- ⮂ Where am I growing in my emotional development? What emotions need more work and focus?
- ⮂ What spiritual growth have I been experiencing lately?

Empowerment: Meditate on your service to others

- ⮂ In what ways am I helping others with their physical health and mindsets?
- ⮂ Who in my life—family, friends, or strangers—would benefit from my special attention toward them?.
- ⮂ What actions can I take to lead people toward healthy thought patterns and mindsets?
- ⮂ What emotions am I observing in others? What role can I play in helping them develop healthy feelings?
- ⮂ How can I spiritually support others in my life?

After this twelve- to twenty-minute silent retreat, write down your thoughts and insights from the experience. This practice prepares you to be present and know which windows and tabs need to be opened and which need to be closed. This meditation practice is also a method of self-coaching.

Something to note here is that you may find you can focus only on one of the pillars during the twelve- to twenty-minute timeframe. That is okay. Tomorrow, you can choose a different pillar to focus on.

BLUE Shirt Leaders recognize the value of silence and inner awareness. They also recognize the importance of being coachable and having the support of others to grow in their self-awareness.

In the next section, we will look at how the coachee habit will unlock new levels of self-awareness and much more.

The Coachee Habit

Every great story has a hero, and every hero has a guide to help them find their way. You can write a great leadership story. But like all heroes, you will also need a guide.

To build powerful self-awareness like a BLUE Shirt Leader, seek coaching and mentorship. The most epic stories have heroes who need a guide to find their way and triumph over the big bad wolf on their journey. You are the hero of your story. Who is serving as your guide?

I hired a coach from Vancouver, Sue, about eighteen months into opening my coaching practice. At first, it felt like a waste of money and time, but Sue and I had a conversation that changed my perspective about needing a guide to help me with my business and my attitudes.

During an impromptu coaching call, I was standing in the middle of my in-laws' kitchen making a sandwich. We started a conversation about what I have to offer my clients and the value I bring.

At that time, I had a low belief in my skills and wasn't valuing my services as I should have. Sue said, "I believe in your potential and ability, Kyle. Do you?" Her question shook me and stopped me mid-sandwich. At the time she asked, the answer was no. Sue asked, "Would you hire you for coaching?"

These were powerful questions. The answer to "Would you hire you?" was a resounding NO. I knew I had the skills, but I didn't believe in my ability to execute. Why would anyone else hire me if I couldn't believe in myself as a coach?

This impromptu coaching call broke through the toxic mindset holding me back from growing my business. Once I was willing to shift my perspective, I quadrupled my coaching fees and watched my clients get more significant results!

In movies and books, we consistently see great heroes get stuck, and they are unable to overcome a struggle, save the day, etc. But then a guide helps them see their potential, shows them how to break through their fears and limiting beliefs, and asks them the right questions to get them back on track.

Since I was a child in the 1990s, Timon and Pumbaa come to mind for Simba in The Lion King, Yoda for Luke in Star Wars, Morpheus for Neo in The Matrix. The point is that each of our heroes needed a guide to help them achieve the ultimate victory. You are the hero in your story. BLUE Shirt Leaders realize this and know they need a guide to help them along the way. In the business world, often that guide is a coach.

To gain the powerful benefits one can receive from coaching, however, you must first be coachable.

■ Four Ways To Be More Coachable

The point of being coachable is for you to shift toward being a better leader. To do this well, here are four suggestions on how to become more coachable.

First, check your ego at the door, and don't make excuses. You don't have it all figured out. Be willing to own mistakes and become vulnerable as you gain new insights into your leadership limitations and strengths. No one wants to be led by someone who doesn't take responsibility or show their flaws.

Second, ask for feedback from colleagues, employees, and coaches. Chapter 8 covers this idea in detail, but coachable leaders continuously adjust based on feedback. Remember that most people in your inner circle want the best for you. Trust them and be responsive to their questions, insights, and critiques.

Third, being coachable requires listening and asking questions. Your questions open possibilities and a path to new thinking. That, in turn, will help you to make the small shifts that create massive change for the future of your leadership and business.

Finally, the full shift toward this habit is to seek a coach that will guide you to becoming the leader you're meant to be

■ Questions To Ponder

- ➲ Who is coaching you now?
- ➲ Would you want to be led by you?
- ➲ What guidance do you need right now in your leadership and business?
- ➲ Would you hire you to do what you do?
- ➲ What mindset is holding you back from fully and enthusiastically believing in yourself?

Pause a few minutes to write your thoughts on these questions in your notes app or journal.

■ Conclusion

There are hundreds of good and bad habits we can develop as leaders. BLUE Shirt Leaders live these five habits—the Platinum Habit, the intuitive habit, the writing habit, the habit of practicing silence, and the coachee habit—daily in their businesses. When you apply the BLUE Shirt Leadership principles and practices, these habits will become second nature.

You will never arrive fully as a perfect leader. Even BLUE Shirt Leaders continue to grow. But one thing is for sure about BLUE Shirt Leaders: They surround themselves with other great people to emulate, be challenged by, and create accountability.

As we continue working through the BLUE Shirt Leadership Framework, accountability is the topic of the following two chapters. You'll learn about the five mindsets of accountability that "GRIPS" the accountability hammer. Then we will discuss a powerful process called the Accountability PASS that helps you achieve 95 percent of your goals!

Ready to supercharge your results with the BLUE Shirt Leadership Framework? Don't wait! Apply now for a consultation with Kyle Gillette and receive personalized guidance to fast-track your success. Take the first step towards transformative leadership.

SCAN HERE

Chapter 5:

———

The Mindsets That Keep Your Leadership House Standing

In the first chapter, you read the story of the Three Little Pigs and the importance of building your leadership house. Through the story, I hope I clarified that you need a solid foundation to build your leadership house upon. You also know that strong nails must hold a well-designed house together. Without these nails, the walls will fall.

The nails of accountability keep your leadership house upright through the power of the five mindsets you are about to learn. These five mindsets are what GRIPS the hammer of accountability. These mindsets are Goals, Responsibility, Integrity, Priorities, and Systems. In the next chapter, we will examine the nails they hammer in. For now, let's focus on understanding the GRIPS mindsets.

Goals Mindset

Researchers from the American Society of Training and Development (ASTD) have found that individuals have the following probabilities of completing a goal by taking these actions:

- ⮑ Thinking of accomplishing a goal: 10 percent
- ⮑ Consciously deciding that you will do it: 25 percent
- ⮑ Deciding on a specific due date: 40 percent
- ⮑ Planning how to do it: 50 percent
- ⮑ Sharing with several people that you will do it: 65 percent
- ⮑ Committing to an accountability appointment with someone: 95 percent

As a business owner, you've probably read a lot about goals and their importance, but I bet these statistics are eye-opening, hopefully in a positive way. This research shows you have a 5 percent chance of NOT achieving your goal by following these steps and creating scheduled accountability with someone!

A 5 percent chance of not achieving your goal is incredible! Intuitively, this makes sense, but would you have guessed that the likelihood of completing a goal would have been in the 95 percent range with just a few simple actions?

■ Achieving Your Business Goals

What goals are you pursuing right now in your business? Do you have clear and measurable goals for the next ninety days, one year, three years, and beyond?

Here's a bit of advice: a goal beyond ninety days typically isn't a good idea to pursue. Why? Too much happens and changes beyond this time frame affect your ability to achieve that goal. But having a *vision* (see chapters 1 and 8) for the future of your business beyond a year is vital! You can think of goals in terms of ninety days and vision as those targets you would like to achieve beyond ninety days.

In this next section, you'll learn the often-used SMART Goals method to achieve goals, but with a simple BLUE Shirt Leadership twist on the process.

For those who have heard of SMART goals, before you roll your eyes and say, "not this again" and want to skip ahead, don't. This twist on the SMART acronym is one you haven't read about, and it's what makes the 95 percent difference.

Here's my version of the acronym.

- ➲ S - Specific
- ➲ M - Measurable
- ➲ A - Accountable
- ➲ R - Results Oriented
- ➲ T - Time-Bound

■ How To Use SMART Goals

Write a simplified version of your goal: Developing the goal within the SMART goal acronym isn't sequential, but you should start by writing out a simple description of the goal. When you write out your goals, it gives a massive boost to your potential success.

Once you've worked through all the SMART letters, you should come back to each specific step and write an even more detailed approach to your goal. Don't skip this last step; it is vital to goal achievement and meaningful accountability.

What big and scary goal do you want to achieve in the next ninety days? Choose something that seems difficult to accomplish and that will stretch you. Once you've written it out in simple form, we will build on that.

Next, create a timeline and commit: Review the goal to get it solidified in your mind, and make a genuine commitment to achieving your goal. The best way to write your goal is this way: I will (commitment) go from "x" to "y" by "date."

Now that you've committed and have a timeline, you've covered the S and T in SMART. The ASTD study mentioned above is about deciding to do the work on the goal. We'll discuss this habit of taking action and its importance in the next chapter.

Measure the goal: The next step, M, is about determining how you will measure your progress in real time and monitor your results. To do this, come up with two or three daily or weekly activities you can do that will lead you to the results you want—more on how to do this when you develop a Job Scorecard.

Tell people: Now tell at least six people your plan to accomplish this goal. When you do this, you're creating what I call passive accountability.

Build your goal plan: At this point, you should have a clear idea of the specific goal and the timing of its completion. You must write out a highly detailed action plan to keep yourself accountable and then share that action plan with your team or accountability partners.

Complete weekly goal check-ins: We must maintain accountability in this process. I have found it best to keep a weekly check-in to review your progress, design your subsequent actions, and hold yourself and your team accountable. These weekly check-ins create a cadence of accountability and should last no longer than twenty minutes. You can do these with a team or on your own. It's the consistency of the check-in that is most important.

From this process, you should have a Specific goal with Measurable indicators. You'll now have Accountability in place to move you toward a clear Result. Finally, all of this is wrapped up nicely with Time-bound check-in meetings and the final date of when the goal is to be accomplished.

■ A Sample Check-In Meeting Agenda

Each team member is to report in a few minutes:

- ☑ Whether they met the previous week's commitments.
- ☑ How well they are moving the lead and lag measures on the scoreboard.
- ☑ What actions can the team member take this week to impact the team's performance on the scoreboard?
- ☑ What new hurdles have come up?

What do you do with a stuck team member?

- ☑ Support them by asking questions. Good leaders ask questions first.
- ☑ Listen well by being intentional in your listening.
- ☑ Keep advising to a minimum and let them discover the solution.

When you follow these steps, you will have created a BLUE Shirt Leadership SMART Goal with a 95 percent likelihood of success.

Here are some questions to ask yourself to help you get started on your first goal.

1. What BIG goal do I want to achieve, and what can I do in the next ninety days to get there?

2. What two or three actions can I take weekly/daily to get the desired results?

3. How can I display progress toward this goal so it is in front of the team and me every day?

4. What day/time will I meet with teammates on this goal?

Write your answers to these questions, and you will be well on your way. The problem often is a failure to create a plan or dashboard, or to design the right actions. Instead, it is taking action that is the problem.

What about your employees? How do you design goals for your employees? The Job Scorecard is the tool to help you empower your employees and keep them accountable to work goals.

■ How To Develop Employee Goals with a Job Scorecard

In my years of coaching and helping organizations hire the right people the first time, I've found that getting the right people is only the beginning of a strong start for new employees. Most small businesses have only a job description for the new hires or sometimes nothing. Once someone is hired, the job description may as well be thrown in the trash because the new employee never looks at it again.

But employees need to know what they are accountable for in their roles. The job scorecard is the tool for creating this accountability context.

You want three things on a job scorecard:

The mission of the position:
The primary objective of the job.

Outcomes for the position:
Primary responsibilities with progress to be made and completion dates.

Lead measures:
Weekly activities that will help the responsible individual take specific actions that lead to the outcomes and mission of the position. These are actions that the person has 100 percent control over. Lead measures are subject to change based on the employee's insights, which is good. When you create scorecards for EVERY position in the organization (including yours), you are building a culture of accountability and iterating your systems in real time. The lead measures help you stick with all five mindsets of accountability and give you an effective way to leverage SMART Goals.

■ A Sample Job Scorecard

VP of Sales, Frank's Painting

Mission: Increase revenue by 50 percent over three years by signing large profitable and repeatable commercial accounts. Hire two employees for the sales department within three years to help grow current accounts and build new business.

Outcomes:

- Grow revenue from $250,000 to $350,000 by the end of year three.
- Decrease residential business by 17 percent by the end of year one.
- Increase commercial accounts from 28 percent to 40 percent by year three.
- Hire one sales employee by the end of year one.
- Stay within 8 percent of quarterly budgets.

Lead measures (100 percent controlled by scorecard holder):

- ➲ Reach out to two local commercial businesses daily to set up sales conversations.
- ➲ Reach out to five commercial contractors weekly to set up networking and referral opportunities.

A benefit of using a job scorecard is that it provides you with three ways to evaluate progress at a glance. The mission is a measurable long-term goal, outcomes are specific indicators of progress made, and lead measures show you real-time progress toward your outcomes and mission.

When you have a job scorecard for every employee, you have an objective way of evaluating their performance. The results of every position can be measured and tracked for improvement and systemization. You, as the leader, can address each employee's performance and measure their progress from an objective perspective.

When these goals and scorecards are in place, your team has their responsibilities clarified and can move forward with confidence.

Responsibility Mindset

When you break down the word responsible, it is simply response-able. It's the idea that you are capable of responding. How many times have you said, "Who's responsible for this?" or "Whose idea was this?" or "Who was supposed to do this?"

■ The Response-Able Donkey

Many years ago, a farmer was working in his fields when he noticed his donkey was missing. He looked for his donkey, only to discover it had fallen into a deep pit. No matter how hard he tried, he couldn't pull it out. So, he decided to bury the donkey alive!

He shoveled soil onto the donkey from above, and every time the donkey felt the load, he shook it off and stepped on it. The more soil the farmer added, the more the donkey shook it off and stepped up. By noon, the donkey was grazing in green pastures.

Both the farmer and the donkey were responsible for this situation. The farmer responded by throwing shovels of soil into the pit. The donkey responded by shaking it off and stepping up.

BLUE Shirt Leaders recognize they are ultimately responsible. They are accountable to themselves, their team, and their clients or customers. They establish a culture of responsibility in their business and life because of their attitude toward accountability.

Do you remember the story I shared about the physical therapist in chapter 3? She was unaware of her responsibility for her business's difficulties. She struggled to have a responsibility mindset needed to make the changes necessary in herself and the company. Though she could *respond* to the situation, she chose not to.

■ What the Responsibility Mindset Looks Like

Start by recognizing it's not about you but everyone else. When you make it about everyone else and not just yourself, people will join in on the responsibility. You'll find allies within your business instead of people who have difficulty wanting to do more than the minimum. Which brings up a question: Why do some people in organizations only do the minimum? Because the leader often blames others and hangs them out to dry instead of supporting them when they need help.

A BLUE Shirt Leader doesn't do this. A BLUE Shirt Leader recognizes the importance of shouldering the blame and taking responsibility. BLUE Shirt Leaders realize the buck stops with them and, at the same time, that it's not about them.

Own the issue. BLUE Shirt Leaders own the mistakes that happen. They recognize that their responsibility is to train, guide, and support the team and, in so doing, take the blame for mistakes.

Taking the blame doesn't mean people aren't held accountable. When a leader makes it clear they will own issues in the business, employees are far more likely to step up and make a lot fewer mistakes.

BLUE Shirt Leaders don't spread blame, they spread accountability.

Deal with issues quickly. Being responsible means dealing with problems quickly. Too many business owners will avoid confrontation with a poorly performing employee or an unpleasant customer. BLUE Shirt Leaders find out all the facts and deal with the situation as quickly and as completely as possible.

BLUE Shirt Leaders recognize that if things are left to fester, they can stink up the business and create far more problems than if they had been dealt with at the start. Because of this, they will do the uncomfortable things and take ownership of the fallout.

Give credit where credit is due. The success of your business depends on the quality of your leadership and your team's performance. BLUE Shirt Leaders recognize their employees' accomplishments. When employees see they are valued, they take responsibility. BLUE Shirt Leaders encourage responsible actions and attitudes.

Confront irresponsible actions and attitudes. A responsibility mindset cultivates a culture of high expectations and quality work. A mindset of responsibility permeates an organization's culture when a business owner demonstrates this through recognition, ownership, and dealing quickly with issues of irresponsibility within the organization.

The responsibility mindset gets at the heart of an accountable leader and business culture. In the following chapter, we'll look at several techniques for developing accountability habits for yourself and others you lead, but here are some questions to consider.

■ Questions To Ponder

- ⊃ When sh!t hits the fan, where does the blame go?
- ⊃ Who is the most responsible person you know? What makes them this way?
- ⊃ Where does the credit go when things turn out well in your business?

As a leader, you are ultimately responsible, but when there's a breakdown in communication or progress has halted, it's often not a lack of responsibility but an integrity problem within your team.

People may not be as honest with you as you may believe. One definition of integrity is "whole or undivided." So when someone fails to give their work the attention it requires, aren't up front when they disagree with you, or flat out lie, integrity becomes an issue.

Unfortunately, as you'll see below, many people don't stick with their convictions (they're divided) and will stretch or hide the truth. The self-aware BLUE Shirt Leader knows the importance of integrity and remains grounded in his or her beliefs and reality. But how do BLUE Shirt Leaders do this?

Integrity Mindset

The central mindset of a self-aware BLUE Shirt Leader is one of integrity. If values are the rebar of your foundation, integrity is the structural fortification of your leadership house.

But what is structural integrity? Structural integrity is "the ability of a structure to withstand its intended loading without failing due to fracture, deformation, or fatigue." It is a concept often used in engineering to produce items that will serve their designed purposes and remain functional for the desired service life.

There will be moments of fracture or breaking down of systems (deformation) and flat-out fatigue during the life of your small business. With an accountability mindset rooted in integrity, you can overcome the battles, struggles, and everything else that comes your way. Whatever the big bad wolves try to break down, the nails of accountability in your Leadership House will hold fast.

■ Abraham Lincoln and Booze

There's a story about Abraham Lincoln traveling in a stagecoach with a colonel from Kentucky. After many miles, the colonel pulled out some whiskey and asked Lincoln to share a drink with him. Lincoln said, "No, Colonel, thank you, I never drink whiskey."

As they continued to travel, they had friendly conversations and enjoyed one another's company. Later, the colonel offered Lincoln one of his cigars. Lincoln said, "You are such a fine and agreeable man to travel with. Maybe I ought to take a smoke with you."

But before he accepts the cigar, Lincoln asks if he could share a story with the colonel. Lincoln said, "My mother called me to her bed one day when I was about nine years old. She was very sick and said to me, 'The doctor tells me I am not going to get well. I want you to promise me before I go that you will never use whiskey or tobacco as long as you live.'"

Lincoln then said, "I promised my mother I never would. Up to this hour, Colonel, I have kept that promise." Lincoln asked, "Now would you advise me to break that promise to my dear mother and take a smoke with you?"

With much emotion, the colonel put his hand on Lincoln's shoulder and said, "No, Mr. Lincoln, I wouldn't have you do it for the entire world. It was one of the best promises you ever made. I would give a thousand dollars today if I had made my mother a promise like that and had kept it, as you have done."

BLUE Shirt Leaders like Lincoln keep their word. Even in what seemed like a trivial situation, Lincoln kept his word. The colonel didn't need to know about the promise. And, as Lincoln's mom had passed away several years earlier, no one would have likely known about the promise.

However, great leaders recognize that their word is their bond. As a result, they hold themselves and others accountable for their words and their actions. Before you get too deeply into this topic, I want to point out that when I write about lying in this chapter, I'm referring to anything from fudging a little in what you say about your business to doing deceitful things to earn a sale or avoid taxes.

Most businesspeople don't do the big things that break integrity in their business, whereas the tiny and easy-to-justify things are more prevalent.

■ Be Impeccable with Your Word

In the Toltec wisdom book *The Four Agreements,* Don Miguel Ruiz describes the integrity mindset as, 'Be impeccable with your word.' In the Bible, Jesus says, "All you need to say is simply 'Yes' or 'No'; anything beyond this comes from the evil one" (Matthew 5:37 NIV).

To be impeccable with your word is the highest level of accountability you can reach. I have a business friend who asked a simple question: "How do you guarantee success?" After thinking about it for a few moments, I said I wasn't sure. After a pause, my friend quietly said, "Do what you say you are going to do."

Always being true to your word is a simple concept, but the application is a different story. A study at UMASS found that 60 percent of people lied at least once during a ten-minute conversation. In a TED Talk entitled, "How to Spot a Liar," Pamela Meyer shares that we're lied to from ten to two hundred times on any given day!

Unfortunately, in business, lying works—in more ways than one. There's an old investment scheme where you send a stock pick to ten thousand people, messaging half the people to buy and the other half to sell.

Inevitably, one of these picks will be correct. The schemer then sends another similar pick to the five thousand who made the right choice. He continues to do this until some prospects have received four or five correct selections in a row. It's easy to close a sale at this point.

Lying creates hundreds of problems for business owners and the people they lead. When a business leader lies, you can be sure that eventually this will become the company's culture. But when a leader demonstrates integrity and is impeccable in their word, the employees will get on board, and so will customers.

The side benefit of the integrity mindset is that it will repel some people who don't fit in a culture with such standards. If you've worked in a culture with an integrity mindset at its core, the caliber of employees and work were likely much higher than in other environments.

A mindset of integrity creates a guilt-free work experience for the BLUE Shirt Leader. They know the promises of their brand, employees, and themselves. There's an expectation set, and it's obvious when it's missed. Being a small business owner of your word also means you don't lie to yourself. Leaders with an integrity mindset follow through with their employees and their customers.

Their business represents this, and their reputations prove it. You can lie about how good OR bad you are at something. You can lie and justify why you did something. You can try to hide things from yourself (and others) to appear the way you want to be perceived by the world. But know that these lies will penetrate your mindset, break down your confidence, hinder new ideas, and limit your potential.

The reasons and schemes are endless when justifying behaviors that break moral principles, but the consequences far outweigh the short-term rewards for a high-integrity BLUE Shirt Leader.

Research reveals that the consequences of not leading from integrity are numerous. For example, lying can lead to an increased risk of anxiety, depression, addiction, and poor work performance. On the relational side, you lose trust with others, and how they value you decreases significantly and will take time to rebuild. How customers, vendors, and prospects deal with you will change forever.

The beauty is the opposite of these consequences is true when you maintain an integrity mindset. You experience more joy, you're able to let go of worries, and performance improves. Trust increases, and challenging situations are easier to deal with. Finally, your bottom line will improve as people see your integrity and want to do business with you.

In one way or another, our integrity is challenged every day. Here are some questions to prepare yourself for that inevitability.

- When was the last time you told a tale or little fib about your business or leadership?

- When you've kept your word in a challenging situation, what was it that made you stay impeccable with your word?

- How can you show an impeccable mindset in your business and create a culture of integrity, honesty, and staying true to your word?

When you keep your promises and have integrity, you take ownership of your words and actions. The payoff of the integrity mindset is multifaceted. Better culture, clearer communication, more effective customer service, and higher-level results usually become the norm for a leader with this mindset.

The big bad wolf will try to take advantage of those little lies or create misdirection to knock down what you have built. But an integrity mindset helps hammer in the nails that keep your leadership house strong and standing upright.

■ Whole and Undivided

Sometimes a business doesn't have a problem with deception. Sometimes the culture is full of honest team members who always follow through on their promises. As you read this, you may know you and your team are true to your word. You may ask, is this mindset principle worth focusing on?

As stated earlier, the definition of integrity is "the state of being whole and undivided." This type of integrity is about communicating completely and thoroughly.

Leaders with integrity not only stay true to their word, but also make sure that their business remains undivided by keeping the goals, responsibilities, priorities, and systems in a state of remaining whole and complete. Within a team with high levels of integrity, there is no bitter division or discord within the team. There may be differences of opinion, but the team remains undivided.

There's a phrase many of us have heard before: "A house divided against itself cannot stand." The origin of the quote is from Matthew 12:25 (NIV): "Jesus knew their thoughts and said to them, 'Every kingdom divided against itself will be ruined, and every city or household divided against itself will not stand.'"

The point is clear. Division that goes on for too long over where you want to go as a leader or where you want the company to go will cause your leadership house to fail. Division at any level or for any length of time will ruin your business.

What I have shared isn't meant to be hyperbolic but to show you that division can come from within you or from within your business. Maintaining an integrity mindset will pound the nails back in. To help you remain strong and build your integrity mindset, you must have your priorities straight.

■ The Dinner Prompts

Recently, we've started to use three prompts at dinner time to encourage reflection and discussion with our kids, who are five, eight, and ten at the time of this writing. The first prompt is, "Today I'm grateful for...." The second is, "Today I served _____ by...." The third is the one that the kids struggle with the most: "Today, I gave my best by...."

These prompts encourage our kids to be purposeful and reflective about how they live their lives. BLUE Shirt Leaders take a similar approach to running their businesses. To have integrity, BLUE Shirt Leaders recognize the need to give their best whenever possible.

During one of our dinner discussions around the table, one of my daughters asked what it means to give your best. I explained that giving your best isn't about the result. I explained, "If in a soccer game you scored three goals but didn't try very hard or have to work hard, and in another game, you put in as much effort as you could but didn't score, which one did you give your best in?"

She said, "The one I scored three goals." We went on to talk about the importance of progress, working hard, and that the result doesn't always reflect trying your best. As she began understanding that the scoreboard is not an accurate reflection of the effort, the same can be true for leading your business. The small habits, the discipline of integrity, and giving your best will set you up for success as the big bad wolf attempts to destroy your hard work.

Priorities Mindset

Just like it is always challenging to give your best, sometimes you will feel somewhat divided or struggle to follow through on your commitments. This struggle is a normal part of being human. The following strategy will help alert you when things are not whole or when they're out of balance. Sometimes we try to nail down the wrong things in our business and our lives. A priorities mindset helps us to focus on the right things.

You may wonder how priorities differ from values (chapter 2). Values are the rebar for your Leadership House. Priorities get moved around a bit. Our values are rooted within us. BLUE Shirt Leaders recognize that every day, week, and season will have circumstances that can easily highjack their progress toward a vision and achieving goals.

When the urgency and day-to-day distractions come along, a priorities mindset limits the amount of pull these situations have on you. Priorities are like big rocks in a river that don't easily move and provide a point of reference for your work and leadership.

If your values reinforce your self-awareness and help you keep the big picture moving forward, your priorities define your work on a weekly and seasonal basis. Goals shift us toward the longer-term priorities we need to focus on, while our values become the compass for achieving our vision.

In his book *The 7 Habits of Highly Effective People,* Stephen R. Covey describes a simple matrix for priorities.

	Urgent	Not Urgent
Important	*Quadrant 1* Crisis "Emergencies" Meetings Deadlines Pressing problems	*Quadrant 2* Planning/Strategy Systems Mindsets Personal Growth Recreation
Not Important	*Quadrant 3* Interruptions Emails Non-urgent calls Other people's problems	*Quadrant 4* Social media Office small talk YouTube Sports

You may get caught up in the tyranny of the urgent. When you feel a bit overwhelmed and can't stay focused on your priorities, the important gets shoved aside by the combination of the urgent and not important. When you feel a bit overwhelmed, sometimes you just want a break and can fall into the trap of focusing on the *not important* AND *not urgent* stuff.

BLUE Shirt Leaders concentrate on spending at least twenty percent of their time in quadrant 2, with sixty percent in quadrant one and the remaining ten in the other quadrants (realistically, even BLUE Shirt Leaders waste some time at work). Be careful that whatever seems *important* and *urgent* doesn't become the default priority for your business and crowds out quadrant 2. If so, the result is poor time management, unclear goals, and not sticking with your word.

■ Sand, Pebbles, and Rocks

A philosophy professor got up in front of his class with an enormous empty glass jar. He filled the jar to the brim with large stones and asked if it was full.

The students all agreed the jar was full.

Next, he added some pebbles to the jar. He gently shook the jar to ensure the pebbles dispersed throughout the jar. He then asked, "Is the container now full?"

The students agreed again that the jar was full.

The professor then poured sand into the jar, shaking the jar again and making sure to get the sand between each rock and pebble. His goal was to fill the remaining space.

The professor then explained that the jar represents your life and business, while the sand, pebbles, and rocks represent the things that have differing levels of importance in your life. The rocks represent the most important projects and things you have going on, such as growing your business, leading well, spending time with your family, and maintaining proper health.

The pebbles represent important things that matter but aren't essential in your life. The pebbles are certain things that give your life meaning (such as your job, house, hobbies, and car), but they are not critical for you to have a meaningful life. These things often come and go and are not permanent or essential to your overall well-being. Nevertheless, they often create the most urgent situations and become the top priority.

Finally, the sand represents the remaining filler things in your life and material possessions, such as watching television, browsing your favorite social media site, or running errands. These tasks are often of low importance and rarely have significant urgency. Although these things don't bring meaning to your life, they can fill our work and lives the most if we aren't careful.

Interestingly, when you remove the pebbles and sand, your jar is still "full."

If you've ever been to the beach, you've likely noticed that sand can get everywhere. Like sand, the less important things in life can fill your business and distract you from the big rocks (priorities) most important to your business.

As you can see, the sand, pebbles, and rocks correspond with the four quadrants. A BLUE Shirt Leader spends most of their time and puts the most importance on the rocks and pebbles of life.

Here's a list of "rocks" for you to focus on. Each category is primarily quadrant 2 activities—not urgent but important.

- ☑ Leadership development
- ☑ Communication
- ☑ Client/customer care
- ☑ Marketing
- ☑ Business strategy

Whether you use this list or come up with your own list, use the following process to help you get your priorities to the place you want them to be.

■ Defining Your Priorities

Take out a piece of paper and write along the left margin five to seven areas of business you are focused on. Title this column "Priorities/Rocks." Leave enough space for three columns next to these categories to do some ranking.

Once you have your five to seven categories, think about how much time you spend on each. In the first column, next to the categories list, write at the top "Reality." Here, rank each item on the list from one to seven in order of how much time you spend on each during a week, with seven being the most.

Next to the "Reality" column, create a new column labeled "Ideal." Then rank your list based on the ideal amount of time you think you should spend on each category in this column.

Finally, label the third column "Delegate." The delegate column is where you decide if you can delegate the area to an employee, freelancer, or vendor. If you can't delegate fully, use "share "here. If you can delegate all of this priority to someone else, add "yes" here.

Priorities/Rocks	Reality	Ideal	Delegate
Marketing the business	3	3	Yes
Networking	4	4	No
Serving clients	6	7	No
Strategic planning	3	4	Share
Busy work of emails, etc.	6	2	No

If you are like most small business owners, your reality and ideal columns won't precisely match. Some leaders need to flip these two columns to give their "rocks" the right amount of time and focus. You may also find you're carrying the "rocks" of someone else and need to get them out of your jar and into theirs.

Too many leaders stay stuck in their heads with all that needs to get done. You may need to do this exercise a few times to get things back on track or hand them off for others to take responsibility. You may want to add this exercise to your daily or weekly activities to help declutter your mind and help you adjust what work needs to be delegated to the right people and resources.

■ Untangling Our Priorities

From time to time, your priorities will get mixed up. We all know to expect mixed priorities in running a business. The problem is when you don't take the time to look at the jar and see how much space the sand and pebbles are taking up in your day. Implementing the priorities exercise into a bi-weekly routine will help keep things from getting too tangled.

With a clear set of priorities, you can perform at a much higher level as a leader. Additionally, clarifying your priorities and allocating correctly will help your team and business function better. With your priorities under control, you can shift to focusing on the systems needed to accomplish your goals. You can see the big rocks through the layers of sand.

Systems give your business a path toward predictable success and growth. The systems mindset keeps your leadership house operating at the highest capacity. Systems keep the lights on, the plumbing working, and everything organized.

Systems Mindset

For an organization to reach its potential, it must have systems in place. The right system will help you attract the right employees, keep the right employees, and increase the productivity of your employees. A system enables you to find new opportunities, make significant decisions, and solve problems that arise from your business.

Maintaining a systems mindset makes life easier as a business owner. Systems also allow you to maintain integrity within your business and keep things to the desired quality standards. It also empowers you to delegate responsibilities, knowing the system will help carry them out. A system mindset also allows you to be flexible, keep the first things first, and maintain your priorities. Finally, your ability to build, support, and improve systems ensures goal accomplishment.

Systems are at the heart of the success of an accountable leader and organization. Systems are at the heart of the BLUE Shirt Leadership Framework.

■ The Five Systems That Every Business Should Have Are:

1. Systems for the growth of the business

2. Systems to grow your people

3. Systems to innovate and adapt faster than your competition

4. Systems that give you more time in your life

5. Systems that allow you to have better customer/client interactions

Write all the actions and processes your business has in place associated with these five basic systems. If you don't have clear processes in place, pause for a moment, and make a note to develop one in the next thirty days. For now, just make a note by briefly describing what you'd like to see, then act and build it!

Each system will require a certain level of consistency and discipline from each person in your organization. It also requires your team to have high integrity and responsibility-centered mindsets.

■ The Power of Business Systems

When processes are in place, and everyone follows them, your company accomplishes its goals, and growth occurs. The systems you develop need to follow your core values. When your systems align with your values and expectations are clear, even in complicated scenarios, decision-making is possible, and progress continues.

You can't plan for everything, but systems will help guide you when the unexpected happens. Your business systems help your employees know the processes to follow in most aspects of your business.

Look back at your priorities list. Within those five to seven rocks, are there clear systems and procedures for people to follow? If not, people within your organization don't know what needs to get done and how to do it. When systems are in place, they help your employees understand what they are accountable for, and things get done.

McDonald's and Chick-fil-A consistently churn out profits, burgers, and milkshakes in predictable ways because of their systems. Remember the job scorecard we talked about? When you apply the job scorecard approach to the goals you set for the business and your employees, you are creating the beginnings of an effective system for each of your organization's priorities and goals.

You can use these scorecards to document how people achieve their goals and build the first version of your operating procedures. As your team gets better and better at accomplishing the goals, your systems will also change and improve. It's a beautiful synergy.

■ Creating Systems To Grow People

For sustained growth and happy employees, create training and procedures that help you grow your people. Start with developing a vision for each position on your team. Share that vision with each team member because when employees know the vision for their role within the team and how they should grow, they are more likely to become the leader you need them to become.

The best way to develop and share this vision is by creating an onboarding program for new employees that combines this vision with the job scorecards. Having a straightforward onboarding program helps the employee understand the company's mission and how they contribute to the overall goal of the company.

It's a good idea to include the following at a minimum on the first day of onboarding:

- A meeting with the business owner to discuss the vision for the company and how important employees are to this vision. The vision is the heart behind what you do.

- A review of the organizational chart that shows whom they report to and the overall company hierarchy.

- A meeting with their supervisor (if it's not you) to review the job scorecard responsibilities and provide them with a procedural manual for their position.

- Provide the employee with a copy of your company's vision and values.

- Build connections for them. Throughout the day, introduce them to people they will work with indirectly and directly.

The rest of the first week includes job shadowing and on-the-job training. Schedule supervisor or owner follow-ups with the newest team members at thirty-, sixty-, and ninety-day intervals to review training progress and answer any questions and/or gain any insights the new employee may have.

■ Why Systems Help You Innovate

When you systematically approach goals and priorities, you can measure what's working and what's not. You can duplicate what is working and innovate to resolve what isn't working.

Most business owners are only guessing when it comes to innovation and changes. They "feel" or "think" their way forward regarding process change. When you use a systems mindset and track what's happening, you KNOW what needs to change and why. For an in-depth discussion on innovation, read chapter 9.

System change occurs best by tracking the progress made on job scorecards and documenting what's working and needs adjustment. Most of my clients do this using a simple spreadsheet, but some use more complicated project management tools. The method you use isn't nearly as important as documenting daily the actions taken toward the outcomes achieved on the job scorecard.

■ How Systems Can Improve Customer/Client Relationships

Systems must work from the inside out for your business to succeed with the people you serve. When you have the first four systems mentioned above dialed in and are constantly innovating, your customers will benefit tremendously.

As customer growth happens, you will find they naturally give you feedback on what they love and don't love. Employees will trust you more and tell you what other things they want from you on behalf of their customers and clients, leading to new ideas, processes, and innovations that benefit the customers and, ultimately, the company.

It's a beautiful feedback loop. But you must remember that the key to these systems being effective is tracking and documenting everything. The best way to do this is through the job scorecard documentation and EPAD. The EPAD process can help you stay focused on the right things and improve efficiency across the board.

■ The EPAD System

While the business needs robust systems, so do you as the leader. Unfortunately, many leaders run their business on autopilot and don't develop time management, communication, or professional improvement systems.

The following acronym is a practical way to help you develop better and better versions of these business and personal systems. This straightforward approach to getting control of your leadership and business is called EPAD. Use it when you're reviewing overall business procedures and reviewing job scorecards. Thanks to Dr. Connor Robertson for this model.

Eliminate:

Eliminate the things you and your business should stop doing. Remove the "extra" or "miscellaneous" actions that prevent your success.

Prioritize:

Determine your priorities. You can regularly use the exercise mentioned above to ensure your personal priorities and business priorities are still aligned.

Automate:

Work to automate your day-to-day work and that of your business as much as possible. Tools such as Todoist, Calendly, and Zapier are great for this purpose.

Delegate:

Delegate that which isn't for you to do. Be careful on this one. It's not what you don't like to do. It's about what doesn't need your attention. Again, reference the priorities exercise in your notes. Most entrepreneurs don't realize how capable their employees are and the burden that would be lifted through smart delegation.

Using EPAD and the job scorecards to evaluate and analyze your systems guarantees significant improvement over time in the results you are getting and a decrease in stress for everyone involved!

■ Systems Give You Freedom

As you focus on developing systems, there are several bonus advantages of having them in place. Employees will have more power to put ideas into action and create new processes within these systems. Employees will also be more likely to produce outcomes that will improve your company, surpass your expectations, and increase employee retention.

With systems in place, you will be more efficient, effective, and productive when making decisions and solving problems. All this will free up your mind to focus on priorities and innovation for you and the business. The higher level of efficiency also allows you to do other essential things such as spend time with your family, work on your business, not in it, and spend time directly developing your employees.

■ Questions To Ponder

↪ What processes do you and the business repeat daily? Weekly?

↪ Describe your business, people, process, and service improvement systems.

↪ What hinders you from having a systems mindset in your leadership and business?

Great systems are monitored, measured, and adjusted to make them as effective as possible. It's beautiful to watch entrepreneurs experience the power of accountability for themselves and their teams. Now that we know the mindsets that GRIPS the hammer of accountability, we shift to the five habits you use to swing the hammer!

Chapter 6:

It Takes a Team to Be an Accountable Leader

In 2015, I decided to write a book based on my experiences of working and living in a men's mentoring program. I didn't fully grasp the monumental challenge this would be.

I learned that writing a book is a serious endeavor, and editing, promoting, and publishing is the most challenging. I'd never written a book before, and I had no clue what I was doing.

Writing a book was a bit of a spur-of-the-moment decision. I remember sitting on the floor in our living room with my laptop, and I just began typing. As I wrote, there wasn't much purpose or direction in what I was writing, but I knew I needed to write.

I wrote *LifeMap - Building a Future When You're Lost in the Present* in Google Docs and periodically shared my progress with my wife. I remember jumping up from the floor, showing her the most recent section I had written, and asking her not to be too critical as she read it. She would smile and encourage me with each new section. Eventually, I started a daily writing routine and worked up an editing plan.

To keep the writing momentum, I engaged friends, family, an editor, and an agent to make the process concrete and remain committed to getting it done. Writing, editing, and eventually publishing my first book all flowed out of five distinct habits of accountability. Those five habits came from years of experience helping the young men in the Alpha Academy become more accountable, as well as from countless books I've read.

I put four of those five habits into a simple acronym to help you remember and apply them. I call this approach the Accountability P.A.S.S. For the remainder of this chapter, we will review how to apply the Accountability P.A.S.S. and create a personal advisory board.

The Passive Accountability Habit

To start, we look at the P in the Accountability P.A.S.S., which stands for passive accountability. There is no specific order to follow, but you will have uncommon accountability when you apply all five practices to your business.

BLUE Shirt Leaders are great at telling stories, sharing their ideas, and selling them. This sharing and telling of stories amount to what I call passive accountability. If you want to increase your chances of success, start with passive accountability.

It took about six months to write the LifeMap book I mentioned above and another six to publish on Amazon. To go from never having written a book to being published required learning new processes, systems, and different types of accountability. As you saw in the ASTD study above, your success rate can rise to 95 percent when you do this right.

Passive accountability is about sharing your dream with others. It's telling the story of where you want to go. It's selling your dream to them and yourself. In my case, it was telling people that I wanted to write a book.

I first started by telling my wife, then the president of Alpha Academy, then several friends and family members. By the time I had written the first few chapters, I'd told at least thirty people. What I told them wasn't simply that I wanted to write a book but that I had a dream of helping thousands of people get their lives on track by creating their LifeMap.

Then the magic happened. After telling so many people about my intentions, people started to ask me how things were going, offered support, and encouraged me. Now I HAD to write the LifeMap book because I didn't want to disappoint all these people.

This passive accountability habit can serve you in many ways and is easy to implement. All you do is share a story about the ideal future you want to create. When I shared the story behind wanting to write a book, I had not only spoken my vision but also engaged a group of people who wanted to help me achieve that vision. Sharing the story behind your goal or dream with others is key to passive accountability.

People care more about you and your goal when you share your story and dreams with them. They tune in and want to know what will happen once you achieve that goal. The truth is that people do care about what you are doing. They just need to be told what you're doing and why. Sometimes, they will follow up with you and ask how things are going with your goal because they want to know the rest of your story. Many want to be part of your story and will help you without asking.

By them freely helping without you asking is what makes the accountability passive. Friends bring it up in passing. They bring it up because they care and want to help you. The result is accountability and potential feedback on your work toward achieving your dream. It's simple and effective.

Passive accountability is the start of this fantastic process. What goal, dream, or vision do you have? Who can you share it with? Whatever it is, solidify in your mind the story behind your goal. What is the deeper connection you have with the goal? For example:

- If you want to take a vacation, why?
- If you want to double your business income, why?
- If you want to serve a new market, why?

Recently, I spoke with a client who hasn't traveled much in his life and would like to visit other areas of the country. During his upbringing, his family didn't have much money, so for him to now be able to leave the country or do an extended summer road trip would have a lot of meaning.

I recently met with another client who is a financial advisor who wants to increase his business revenue significantly—but the reason behind this wasn't what you might expect. He wanted more disposable income to serve the homeless in his area.

Regardless of the goal, find the why. Think about the reasons behind your goal and what achieving it would mean for you.

I would like you to stop reading right now and write out the goal and the why behind the goal, then make a list of twenty people you can share the goal with and why this goal is essential to you. Twenty people might sound like a lot, but it's easier than you think to spread the word. Storytelling is done best in person or over the phone. Use one of these methods when you tell people what you're up to in your business.

Your next step in creating accountability is actively enlisting people to support you on your journey.

The Active Accountability Habit

I have a friend named Shawn who came into the Alpha Academy program while I was a leader. Shawn was very broken and struggling with life when I first met him. A schizophrenic mom, emotional abuse as a child, and his history of drug addiction made his life rather challenging.

When Shawn came into the program, he had some excellent job skills. He was a welder, mechanic, and handyman, too. His goal was to get off drugs, attend college, and have a "normal" life. This goal became his LifeMap.

I still remember the glassy-eyed look on Shawn's face during our first few meetings and how he would disappear into another place in the middle of a conversation. It was like his operating system would freeze up from time to time.

After months of being in the program and having daily conversations and accountability sessions, he started to change. The effects of the drugs were wearing off, and his brain and body were healing.

Despite all his confusion and lost focus, the team could see Shawn was a brilliant man. His mechanical aptitude shone brightly, along with his curiosity and hardworking nature. Shawn was the type of person who always needed people to be there to bounce ideas off and to support him.

During the program, he started going to a community college, and shortly after he left the program, he found a welding job. He is such a talented welder that he came in second in a national welding event in Hawaii. Yep—there is such a thing.

Eventually, Shawn would come back to the program not only as a house leader but as a mechanic and handyman. Throughout his time at Alpha Academy, he would meet weekly with me, the president of the program, or another volunteer, and sometimes more than one of us in a week.

During these purposeful conversations, having the active accountability habit kept him on track more than he could have on his own. With active help, when he would deviate from his plan, we would let him know the check engine light was on, and he would get back to his plan.

Over time, Shawn fell in love with a woman, found work at a refinery, bought a house, and married. Still, throughout this process, Shawn would reach out to the team and connect at least once or twice a month.

Shawn told me that without the program and the continued support he wouldn't be where he is now. His story is a story of the power of accountability and commitment. Sure, Shawn experienced hiccups along the way, but because of the constant phone calls, lunches, and purposeful support Shawn received, he overcame those challenges.

Shawn's story exemplifies the "A" in the Accountability P.A.S.S.

■ How You Can Use Active Accountability

Active accountability entails purposefully asking two or three people in your life or business to connect with you weekly or biweekly to discuss your progress toward your goals. Active accountability is not a new idea. It is the foundation of Alcoholics Anonymous, churches, and other contexts. It works for the growth of your leadership, too.

Here's how to start. Write a list of three to five people you trust and know care deeply about you. Then reach out to them and ask them individually if they can meet with you twice a month to discuss your growth as a leader and your goals.

In return for them agreeing, offer the same active accountability to them. This one action bumps you to that 95 percent success rate. But you must commit and be consistent. More on the habit of commitment later.

I've used the active accountability approach to write the LifeMap book, start this business, create an app, keep my business open during a pandemic, and build an incredible marriage!

You can magnify the impact of both passive and active accountability habits by putting purposeful structures in place to hold yourself accountable.

The Structures Habit

What is the structures habit? The first "S" in P.A.S.S. is structures. The goal is to construct or arrange a plan and establish a pattern or organization. The structure habit helps keep you, your team, your business, and your life in order and structured as YOU desire.

Your smartphone is the most straightforward tool to create the structure you need to maintain accountability. As a warning, there are some statistics you need to know and some steps you should take to use this tool most effectively for accountability.

Some statistics say that the average smartphone user gets between forty and sixty push notifications daily. If you are awake for an average of sixteen hours a day, you will receive 2.5–3.75 notifications every hour. Most of these will occur in the middle of your working day, constantly interrupting your workflow.

If you're like most entrepreneurs, you probably could go with fewer notifications/alerts on your phone. So, before you move on, read through this list of notifications you don't really need.

- Emails
- Social media apps
- News
- Sports
- Music
- Podcasts
- Games

If you are honest with yourself, you don't need these notifications. Without these notifications, you're still going to check your email (you're probably addicted), you're also going to check sports scores and listen to your favorite song or podcast as you need without this automation. Missing a social media or game ping will not change your life. We also know that watching the news is a painful experience and should be done in limited amounts.

Some business owners I have worked with have even turned off text notifications and WhatsApp notifications. If you want to be present, stay self-aware, be highly accountable, and keep growing, consider turning off as many notifications as possible.

The statistics show that 66 percent of us are addicted to our phones. These statistics do not make phones bad, but we must be wise in how, when, and why we use our devices. With the structure part of the Accountability P.A.S.S., you are taking back control of your habits, primarily around how you use your phone.

The only notifications on my phone are my text messages, phone calls, and calendar alerts. That's it! A few apps have badges only if they have a message feature. By turning off notifications, I have become less stressed and more focused.

It is glorious. Now, I'll be set if you can help me rid myself of my YouTube and Netflix addictions.

Before you move on, be bold and turn off as many notifications as possible.

Did you do it?

Good for you!

I recently had a conversation with a client who was very distracted by Facebook as we talked. He runs a nine-figure real estate business, and the notifications and distractions felt like "ten thousand pounds" on his shoulders.

I asked, "What can you do about this?" He wasn't sure. I asked, "Can you delete Facebook?" He said, "I guess so."

I then challenged him to delete it right then and there. After asking if I was serious, he hesitantly said okay, picked up his phone, and deleted Facebook. Right after, he said he felt five thousand pounds lighter.

These distractions prevent us from being more effective and using the powerful tool we carry daily most effectively. If you still haven't taken the bold action, take a moment and reference the list above and turn off those notifications.

Now that you've finally done that, below are a few additional tools and processes to help you create accountability in your life.

■ Digital To-Do List

This is the crucial structure-creating app. It is the seventh lobe of my brain. The creator of the Getting Things Done method has said, "Your mind is for having thoughts, not keeping them." His perspective may seem extreme, but the idea is to get rid of the stupid stuff and trust the structures you've put in place to help you accomplish things.

My to-do list weapon of choice is Todoist. If a task is on the list, there is an extreme probability I'll get it done, even if it's a crappy thing like cold-calling, detailed work, or setting up a meeting I don't want to attend.

This tool creates structure around the things that need to get done, tracks them, alerts you (though I don't use notifications), and is an excellent reference for ideas and future tasks. Additionally, this tool allows you to forget the little things that need to be done and trust the task to pop up on the list at the right time. Invariably, they do, and then you can get it done.

■ Digital Calendar

A digital calendar is vital for maintaining structure. I can't tell you how many times a calendar notification has saved me from being late to an appointment or missing it altogether. These are notifications worth leaving on.

Calendar notifications remind you to go to meetings, leave on time for things, and start a particular task for accountability purposes. They can also remind you to shift your thinking to the new mindsets and habits you want to create.

Last, I use my Google Calendar to color code my quadrant 2 work to ensure I'm allocating the right hours to seven categories I've deemed as my big rocks. I encourage you to color-code your categories and calendar this way. It's all about tracking yourself and building systems to see progress.

■ Pen and Paper

Another tool that helps keep you accountable is writing your goals and intentions on paper. If you want to see something improve, achieve something big, or break a destructive habit/mindset, write it on various pieces of paper.

Next, take those sheets of paper and put them in places you will see throughout the day. These aren't simple sticky-note reminders. These notes should have big things that matter in your life and business.

The principle here is that if you want to achieve your goals, you must have a relationship with them. To have a relationship with someone or something, you need to be in contact with them.

BLUE Shirt Leaders know the power of structure and deploy it in dozens of ways in their leadership and life. These three structures have changed my life and business, along with the lives and businesses of all the entrepreneurs and leaders I've coached. Here's a list of several more ideas you can use to build accountability.

- Build a new habit on an old one. Example: Add a new habit to your morning coffee routine.
- Email yourself reminders.
- Make sure sticky notes are close at hand.
- Use acronyms and alliteration to help you remember important habits.
- Schedule the call, meeting, or flight before you're ready. This helps hold you accountable.
- Prep for the "thing" the day before.
- Create a contract with your accountability partner.
- Plan to reward yourself once you accomplish a goal.
- Post a video on social media telling people what you plan to do.

Your goal is to choose the best tools to remain committed to your plans and dreams. When you put specific structures in place, you will reap the benefits of less stress, better follow-through on your commitments, and a better understanding of what you can accomplish in a day, week, or beyond.

The Self-Commitment Habit

There's a story about three frogs sitting on a log looking at some beautiful lily pads floating in the water. They were all sitting there for some time, staring at the lily pads. After several minutes, two of the frogs decided they would jump onto a lily pad.

Here's my question. How many frogs are on the log now? Did you say one frog? If you did, you're wrong. There are still three frogs sitting on the log. The two decided to do something. However, they didn't commit to taking action.

When an athlete is flying through the air or going insanely fast, and there's no turning back, at this moment, they cannot stop their momentum. The commitment is complete. Commentators will say, "He's committed now." There is an action in any task/goal/habit where you truly commit—that moment where you can't go back.

To be sure, you must decide to do something, but you haven't committed until you've taken that step of no return. Until then, there isn't enough follow-through on the decision yet.

Think about it this way. Have you ever gone skydiving? Even if you are in the plane and the light is green for jumping, you're still not committed. You may have decided to skydive, but the commitment starts when you step out of the plane.

It's in that moment when you put your hands on the outside edge of the plane and feel the wind in your face that you are getting close. Then you begin to lean out the door. You still haven't reached the point where you cannot climb back into the plane. It is when gravity takes that you hit the point of no return. When you find that point, you are fully committed.

A trick to helping you achieve this is to imagine yourself in a situation where you've reached that point of no return. Now reflect on what that looks like for this particular goal. What does it feel like? Now leverage that information to help you with your self-accountability.

Self-commitment entails acting on your decision. Have you ever attempted to plunge into ice-cold water before? There comes a moment in your mind when you decide that you will do it despite how insane it might seem. Commitment happens when you bend at your knees, pull your arms back behind you, and jump.

At that point, gravity wins and you've committed. Where in your business and leadership do you need to hit that point where gravity takes over? Where you let go of control and plunge in. This idea is the second S in P.A.S.S.: self-Accountability—deciding and then committing to yourself that you will follow through.

Here are a few areas that you could commit to that point of no return:

- ⊃ Commit to yourself
- ⊃ Commit to following through on what you started
- ⊃ Commit to your word
- ⊃ Commit to not quitting
- ⊃ Commit to risk
- ⊃ Commit to success
- ⊃ Commit to growth
- ⊃ Commit to others

⮕ Commit to empower

When you make these commitments, you demonstrate a self-accountability mindset. You are challenging yourself and everyone around you when you maintain the habit of commitment.

Even with the Accountability P.A.S.S., putting your money where your mouth is can be hard. No matter how many reminders, to-do lists, or people you inform, it's challenging to get started and finish the task.

Before moving to the fifth accountability habit, take out your notes again.

■ Let's Put P.A.S.S. To Work Right Now

Begin by writing out your goal with a due date in your notes. Use the commitment and accountability sledgehammer to nail this objective to the wall. Here are the steps:

1. Write your goal with a due date.

2. Make a list of at least twenty people you can talk to about this goal.

3. Make a list of three to five people you could ask to meet with you weekly or biweekly to discuss your progress on goals.

4. List five to seven structures you could use to help keep you accountable for accomplishing this goal.

5. Create a contract on paper to build the necessary self-commitment to this goal.

Remember, the big bad wolf is always there, trying to stop us from achieving our objectives. The winds of fear, failure, lack of information, and analysis paralysis are the wolf's way of knocking down our goals. But you won't have to worry if you've constructed your leadership with the BLUE Shirt Leadership Framework.

The Advisory Board Habit

Having a team to support your big goals and dreams is why the fifth accountability practice is so essential—the habit of keeping an advisory board.

Do you remember movies with a lone cowboy? The cowboy tries to take on the world by himself—just him and his horse on prolonged journeys into the wilderness with no contact with the outside world. This is supposed to portray the ideal of a "manly man," except that's not even remotely true. Life isn't supposed to be a solitary experience. Life is a team sport, not a single-player sport.

No one attains anything by themselves.

I wouldn't be a college graduate, I'd be addicted to who knows what, and I am sure I wouldn't be married with kids if it weren't for the individuals in my life that have kept me on track.

> *You live on the promises or broken promises of those who came before you.*

In the same way, your word and your follow-through will affect those that come after you. Like it or not, we depend on one another in life and business.

You need others for many things, including support, encouragement, and success. And when it comes to success, you especially need others for accountability.

You need to be accountable not only for what you do but also for what you don't do. Without accountability, you can't get to where you want to go in business. You can't live up to your potential and will often settle for "good enough" without some level of accountability.

In my experience, running a business with accountability is a far more gratifying experience. While accountability revolves around keeping your promises, it also involves the people you choose to be connected to your business.

Accountability is like the check engine light in your car, but for your life and business. The check engine light tells you when you have a problem but does not fix it. Creating an advisory board is a highly constructive approach to creating accountability and gaining wisdom for your business. They are your check engine light.

In 2016, I did just that. I flew from Seattle, Washington, to Orlando, Florida, for a week-long intensive certification with John Maxwell. After the week, I decided I wanted to get him on my board of advisors, so I did.

After John was on board, I added a consultant named David Fields. Following David, I ensured my wife was on the board and two other friends were. Finally, I wrapped it up with Andy Andrews.

My board is a powerhouse of advisors. Eventually, I removed John and David and replaced them with Dr. Caroline Leaf and Karen Kimsey-House.

If you're in the world of leadership, you may recognize John Maxwell's name. If you do, you know how big of a deal it was to have him on my board. But did John *really* sit at a table and advise me? No. But his books, courses, and speeches did. The same can be true of your board members that aren't mentors, friends, or your spouse.

The value to developing your personal board of advisors is that they can be alive or dead, aware or unaware of their seat on the board, and you may remove them at any time and still achieve massive growth.

The ideal board consists of three or four individuals with whom you are familiar and can have regular conversations, along with one or two people who are gurus outside your circle of influence.

My board now has a few business acquaintances, a business mentor, and a coach. Outside of personal connections, I'm giving a lot of attention to Michael E. Gerber of E-Myth fame.

Jim Rohn famously said, "We are the average of the five people we spend the most time with."

So, who are you spending most of your time with? Is it the actors on your favorite TV show? Is it the talking heads on the news? Your spouse? Friends?

When you become conscious of whom you choose to spend most of your time with, your accountability and self-awareness will improve. To help you do this, answer the following questions in your notes.

- Who do you spend the most time with in the entertainment world?
- Who's on your relationships board?
- Who do you get advice from about your finances?
- Who advises you on your health? Fitness?
- Who helps guide your business decisions?

In all areas of life and business, people and things are constantly advising you. The greater control you have over who and what is sitting on your board, the more likely you are to achieve your objectives and find success.

The method to build your board is like what you will use with the active accountability partners. Figure out who your three or four members are that you know, and then begin to reach out to them regularly for their input.

Also, take the time to observe other successful people and learn from how they raise their families, run their businesses, stay fit, etc. The goal is to become purposeful in getting advice through conversations or observations.

■ Don't Let the Nails of Accountability Loosen

Below are tactical ways to help you implement the things you are learning. These are five things you can do to maintain accountability in your leadership and business.

1. Sign a commitment contract addressed to yourself.

    ⮑ Put it where you can see it all the time.

    ⮑ Share it with the people you have active accountability with.

    ⮑ Email it to yourself and set the delivery for a week from when you signed it.

    ⮑ Mail it to someone else and challenge them to sign a commitment contract.

    ⮑ Mail it to yourself.

2. Join A Right Now Mastermind

I host bi-weekly masterminds for business owners fighting through the overwhelming confusion of small business ownership. You will likely find some people you can add to your board in these groups. Visit blueshirtcoaching.com/mastermind to apply to join a group.

3. Start implementing the Accountability P.A.S.S. now!

    ⮑ Reference the five-step process above regularly.

    ⮑ Engage other people in utilizing the Accountability P.A.S.S.

4. Ask great accountability questions of yourself.

    ⮑ What am I committing to in this situation?

    ⮑ What role did I play in this not working?

- What can I do to make changes within myself here?

- What mindset do I need to change in me?

5. Finally, hire a coach as a success partner. Here's what they should provide you:

- Keep you accountable to your commitments.

- Make more significant commitments.

- Strategize with you to solve future problems.

- Hold you to account for inaction and excuses.

- Call you out on your BS.

The buck stops with you as the leader. You will succeed when you use the Accountability P.A.S.S. and build a board of advisors that serve as your check engine light and help you not do it alone.

The possibilities of what you can accomplish drastically change when you employ the skills taught in this chapter. Now that you've laid the groundwork and have accountability tools, you can reliably apply the growth mindsets and habits in the following two chapters.

Ready to supercharge your results with the BLUE Shirt Leadership Framework? Don't wait! Apply now for a consultation with Kyle Gillette and receive personalized guidance to fast-track your success. Take the first step towards transformative leadership.

SCAN HERE

Chapter 7:

How Badly Do You Want To Grow As a Leader?

A boy once asked a wise old man about the secret to success. After thinking about the question, the wise man told the boy to meet him at the lake in the morning, and he would answer his question then.

The following day, they met and began walking directly toward the water. The boy was confused when the man stepped into the water, asking the boy to join him. Suddenly, the old man pushed the boy under the water and held him there.

The boy worked as hard as he could to get a breath. As he struggled to get out from under the water, the man continued to hold him underwater. Eventually, the man let go of the boy so he could breathe. The boy gasped as he inhaled a deep breath of air.

After the boy caught his breath, the man asked, "What were you fighting for when you were underwater?" The boy gasped, "To breathe!" The man said, "That is the secret to success. You will obtain it when you want success as much as you wanted air when you were underwater."

As dramatic of an illustration this is, the point is clear. We've all been in situations as leaders where we were desperate for air. We did anything we could to fill our lungs again. BLUE Shirt Leaders need to grow their ability to lead and influence others like they need air to breathe.

You'll need to grow as a leader in significant ways to achieve your dream. If your current skills and abilities can get you to your dream, your dream isn't big enough. A leader with big dreams inspires others to follow. A leader with small goals doesn't inspire followers.

Leaders have dreams they need to grow into. But there is a cost to growing. The cost is taking intuitive and smart risks in your leadership and sometimes experiencing failure and pushback from others. That is why the first growth mindset of a BLUE Shirt Leader is the risk mindset.

Becoming the leader you're meant to be is not a straight-line process. The big bad wolf may try to smash some windows, burst through your front door or intimidate you into stopping. When the risks you take don't work out as expected, they can either crush your motivation or spur you on to fight even harder for that "air" you need.

Risk Mindset

Great leaders recognize they need to have a risk mindset. They understand that taking intelligent risks is often the way to success. Sometimes those risks you are thinking of taking don't feel too bright, but your gut is telling you to take it.

Whether the risks you take in business are intuitive or calculated, you need to get no's to understand what's possible. Developing a risk mindset helps you try things that may look like they will work out the first time because you know that no matter the outcome, there is always a payoff. When you take intelligent and scary risks, you open the door to explore new things you never have before.

Finally, when you take risks, you show others that smart risks are valued in your organization. Mistakes will inevitably happen if you challenge others to do something that requires risk. As a leader, you must be willing to build risk into all aspects of your process and accept the risk that others take within your business.

Most importantly, when others take intelligent risks, BLUE Shirt Leaders encourage them for their efforts. When you do this, you and your team think with a risk mindset and generate significant opportunities.

Every leader will have different tolerance for risk. Some risks don't produce the results you seek and will bring failure. With a growth mindset, the failures will be turned into learning opportunities, as you will see with the learner's mindset.

Having a risk mindset allows BLUE Shirt Leaders to maintain the learner mindset. But to get there, you must be willing to risk and fail. It may sound like taking risks would not be something good to focus on. But trust me, there are some benefits, such as:

- ⮑ When the risk results in failure, you learn to get up and try again.

- ⮑ Taking risks leads to a deeper understanding of your limitations and strengths, building your character and integrity.

- ⮑ Taking risks and learning from them gives you the confidence to know it's not too big a deal to fail and realign what's most important.

- ⮑ Taking risks and learning from the results clarifies where you are and how much further you need to go.

- ⮑ The risks a leader takes often result in innovation and courage.

However, none of these benefits will happen if you don't start with a willingness to risk. What a risk mindset looks like is pushing yourself, your team, and your business into unfamiliar territory—and in doing so, mistakes happen.

■ Four Businesses, Two Successes

As I shared in chapter 2, the failure rate of small businesses is high. Your goal is to push yourself, your process, and your team to stress test to a failure point. A risk mindset looks like failure in reasonable quantities. However, for some, a full-blown business closure (or two) is needed to push you forward.

After graduating from college, I wanted to start a personal training business. I lived with a roommate in San Luis Obispo, California. We spent much time enjoying the sun, the beach, and being active. But it's not cheap to live in San Luis Obispo, so I pursued personal training to earn money and still enjoy an active and fit lifestyle.

I received my personal training certification and began working with clients at a Mixed Martial Arts (MMA) gym and tennis club. Success came quickly, and I enjoyed my life and my work. The business was a dream come true.

The income I generated was enough to live and have a bit extra to save up. I had a great client. Heck, I trained an MMA fighter and helped some locals improve their tennis game while assisting many others to lose weight. *Business number one: success.*

After about eighteen months, I stepped away and returned to the men's mentoring program I mentioned previously. Eight years later, my wife and I moved to Washington state to be closer to her family. It was a great move, but I was at a loss for my next career step.

When we moved to Bellingham, Washington, I applied to dozens of jobs before beginning work as a senior living facility director. I've always had an entrepreneurial spirit, and although I was grateful to be working, I started developing an online personal training business. The business offered customized workouts based on my client's specific health and fitness goals. I designed custom workouts and helped my clients implement the training into their daily lives.

Unfortunately, I thought just putting up a website and adding a few blog posts would get me the attention I needed to be successful. It didn't. This business was a complete waste of time and money because I put minimal effort into outreach and promotion.

This was my "If you build it, they will NOT come" moment. In the service-based businesses, it requires much more effort to get people to sign up for your services than creating a Facebook ad. The truth is, I didn't want to commit to this reality; I wasn't willing to risk leaving my full-time job and going all in. The poor results spoke for themselves. *Business number two: closed.*

Despite this business closure, I learned a valuable lesson. Every successful business brings value, does direct outreach, and consistently networks. Just because you have a website and post some stuff on social media doesn't mean you will get clients.

After the director position at the senior living facility, I got the bug in 2015 to begin writing my LifeMap book, and this started business number three. I thought I had it all figured out. I combined all the lessons I had learned in my previous businesses and started earnestly to work to develop my life coaching and personal development business, called LifeMap Coaching.

Even to this day, I believe this business has a chance. I applied my newly learned marketing and networking skills to promote what I was doing. My writing skills were evolving so that I could write my book. I learned how to overcome my fear of public speaking. All this growth led to publishing a book and workbook based on LifeMap Coaching and even hosting a few workshops on the LifeMap concept.

Things weren't progressing as quickly as I had hoped with my LifeMap program. But again, my commitment wasn't what it needed to be. I didn't want "air" badly enough. In this case, I was too afraid to risk stepping away from a comfortable job. This unwillingness to risk proved to be the demise of the business. *Business number three: closed.*

What I realized about this business is that I didn't have a true passion or vision behind what I was doing. Because of this, I didn't fight hard for success. As you think about your business successes and the risks you've taken to get where you are, I want to encourage you to learn from the achievements and remind you of what you probably already know. There are no shortcuts. My next story illustrates this truth very well.

As I sit at my computer, I'm a happy man with Right Now Business Coaching moving along smoothly, and with God's help, we've had a yearly revenue increase of at least 34 percent. It looks like *business number four is a success.*

The key difference between businesses one and four vs. two and three was my willingness to take risks and, as one of my clients says, "Suck it up, buttercup." This risk mindset helped in the initial months of the COVID pandemic that saw the business drop in revenue by 75 percent. The risk mindset helped me write this book, develop an app, and successfully grow the business each year despite the hiccups. This risk mindset gives me hope that on the other side of the risk are great opportunities, as is often the case.

What about you? Do you have a risk mindset? Write three to five bigger risks and the main lessons you learned in taking that risk. Take a moment and celebrate the courage you had to take that risk. It will make you stronger when you take risks and bump into a failure or even have a business close, as I did! Without those experiences and the associated mistakes and failures, I know I wouldn't be where I am today.

■ The Butterfly Cocoon

One day, a girl saw a butterfly trying to escape from its cocoon. She patiently watched the butterfly struggle for hours to break free from the cocoon. At one point, it seemed like the butterfly would never escape. The butterfly stopped moving–it appeared to be stuck.

So, the little girl decided to help get the butterfly out. She went home to get a pair of scissors to cut open the cocoon. The butterfly could easily escape the cocoon after she cut a little slit. As the butterfly sat and spread its wings, the little girl noticed how wrinkled they were and soon realized that the butterfly could never fly.

Without the struggle to escape, the butterfly didn't gain the strength needed to fully develop and fly. You are like the butterfly. The battle is part of the process required to build your leadership and help those you lead soar fully.

The girl still thought she had done the butterfly a favor. However, the butterfly could not fly and could only move by crawling with tiny wings and a large body. The girl was sad to see this and knew the butterfly would never fly.

BLUE Shirt Leaders recognize that taking a risk and experiencing setbacks is fundamental to strengthening their leadership resolve and preparing them for future challenges. When this mindset permeates a business, it sets it up to be resilient and face challenges with courage, wisdom, and creativity. Without the struggle, you and your business will not fly.

Without adopting a risk mindset, I wouldn't have been able to help my clients make more money and be bolder in their vision for their lives and business, and I'd still be looking for an easy way to succeed. That doesn't really exist.

Maybe you hear people telling you to give up. Perhaps you tell yourself, "Give up, don't risk it. I've made too many failures and mistakes." But this struggle of confidence and certainty is the cocoon you are in. These personal and professional struggles shape us into BLUE Shirt Leaders when we embrace them and choose to learn from them.

Choosing to develop a learner's mindset is precisely the mindset you'll learn about next. But only if you're willing to take some intelligent risks. A learner mindset is a way to get the most from mistakes.

Learner Mindset

The first year my wife and I had a garden in our backyard, we did many things right, and as you can imagine, many things were wrong. I built garden boxes and added great soil to them. We planted the seeds at the right time and watered them well.

We were off to a great start, but there were a few things we didn't do so well. We sort of picked random seeds to plant, like kale. Why did we choose kale? I have no idea; we don't even like kale. We also put too many seeds in the rows and didn't take the time to thin our crop.

From the surface, the garden appeared to be doing well. But as the season went on, we had too many vegetables and had things rot on the vine. We took these lessons to heart.

In the second year, we decided to think both long-term and short-term. We added some red potatoes and some asparagus to our garden that year. We had a bad harvest despite learning some lessons from the previous year. But as you'll see, this was entirely our fault.

Regarding gardening, we didn't have good habits in place. For example, we weren't consistently watering and weeding! To successfully grow thriving plants, you must be purposeful with the soil, watering, planting, thinning, and weeding. We could have done a much better job of this.

The third-year garden was going to be our successful year. We not only remembered the lessons learned but did something with the information—we applied it. We were learning and applying. As a result, some amazing things happened. The asparagus grew, the potatoes took off, and the garden did much better.

Our harvest was much better once we learned from our mistakes.

A learner's mindset is like growing a garden. Your relationships, actions, and attitudes need tilling, planting, thinning, watering, and harvesting. Not just once but consistently. But if you don't remain diligent, sometimes healthy plants can become tangled with weeds, and removing the weeds will harm the healthy plant!

In your leadership garden, sometimes it can look a little dry. You may need to do more watering (create new opportunities, get the support you need, etc.) to help your leadership flourish again. Sometimes, you need to turn the soil over and add some new, healthy soil (adjust the environment, let some employees go). Other times, you will thrive and need to take on new responsibilities and risks to continue your growth and thrive.

When you look back at your entrepreneurial experience, you've likely had experiences like my first-, second-, and third-year gardens. There were both healthy and unhealthy people in each season, positive and negative situations, and different opportunities. How did you manage this? What did you learn from these seasons?

There's a simple, five-question method you can use to maintain a learner's mindset and create a flourishing garden.

In your leadership, every weed you pull (negative outside influences), every plant that gets thinned (destructive mindsets or habits), every new seed you plant (ideas and creativity), and every time you water or till your soil (improve your environment), you make changes that will help you progress toward BLUE Shirt Leadership. You need the right tool to take care of your learner mindset garden. One of the most effective tools you can use is called the MOLO.

The "More or Less of" (MOLO) questions help you determine what behaviors, values, strengths, or weaknesses you need to address. Then, use the information gained from the answers to build powerful habits that will give you the best opportunity to improve your business and leadership.

■ The Five Questions to Answer:

1. What should you do more of?
2. What should you do less of?
3. What should you start doing?
4. What should you stop doing?
5. What should you keep doing?

Reflect on these five questions at the start or end of your week. Answering these simple questions will help you maintain growth in your business and allow you to reflect and learn from your experiences.

There are several areas of your business to which you can apply this reflective exercise. The key to the process is to take only one topic at a time. Some suggestions include:

- Marketing a specific service or product
- Monday staff meetings
- First-time customer interactions with staff
- Hiring practices for a new position
- Professional development of yourself

Answer all five questions focused only on the topic you choose. The method loses effectiveness if you choose more than one topic at a time and give multiple answers.

Last, ensure your responses to these questions are action-oriented so you can act on them. At the end of the exercise, you should have a maximum of five actions. I personally generated many ideas and actions from this method, so I recommend sticking with only one action per question—any more than this will feel overwhelming.

Once you determine your actions, add them to Todoist or whatever tool you use.

The MOLO is a game-changer for leaders. There is no end to how effective and beneficial this weekly exercise can be. Completing this weekly exercise has helped many of my clients generate thousands of dollars in revenue, reduce stress, and get organized.

Take time now to list five to seven topics you can filter through these questions. You will quickly find yourself weeding out the distractions and harvesting what works best in your business in no time.

In the next section, we learn the importance of persistence in growing your leadership and business.

Persistent Mindset

Persistence means to continue a course of action despite difficulty or opposition. A persistent mindset is an attitude of heart and mind that understands difficulty and opposition. From day-to-day tasks to the long-range plan of your business, you will find resistance, but a mindset of persistence will help you be the leader you're meant to be and grow your business to where it is supposed to go.

One man is credited with writing over 28 percent of the New Testament. Within the Apostle Paul's writings, we learn of his trials, tribulations, and perseverance. In leadership, persistence is one of the most critical mindsets. Everyday leaders experience setbacks, rejection, and resistance in many forms. When you learn about Paul's story, you'll find he is the ultimate example of persistence in the New Testament.

After Paul's conversion on the road to Damascus, his zeal for God caused him to face many trials and persecutions. However, he persisted in sharing the gospel and staying on mission, no matter the cost. Paul's persistence is a significant reason the world knows the gospel today. He detailed his hardships in 2 Corinthians 11:24–29 (NIV):

Five times I received from the Jews the forty lashes minus one. Three times I was beaten with rods, once I was pelted with stones, three times I was shipwrecked, I spent a night and a day in the open sea, I have been constantly on the move. I have been in danger from rivers, in danger from bandits, in danger from my fellow Jews, in danger from Gentiles; in danger in the city, in danger in the country, in danger at sea; and in danger from false believers. I have labored and toiled and have often gone without sleep; I have known hunger and thirst and have often gone without food; I have been cold and naked. Besides everything else, I face daily the pressure of my concern for all the churches. Who is weak, and I do not feel weak? Who is led into sin, and I do not inwardly burn?

Paul was ...

- ⮌ Repeatedly imprisoned
- ⮌ Flogged
- ⮌ Faced death again and again
- ⮌ Received thirty-nine lashes five times
- ⮌ Beaten with rods three times
- ⮌ Pelted with stones
- ⮌ Shipwrecked three times

Paul had a clear goal and focus. Paul was a leader that was all in. As a leader, you will have many demands on you, but to lead at the highest level, you must persist in leading like a BLUE Shirt Leader.

In many ways, Paul embodied the idea of having nothing to lose and everything to gain. He said, "For to me, to live is Christ and to die is gain" (Philippians 1:21 NIV). This may seem extreme, but there's a leadership lesson here.

When you look at Paul's life, he worked toward a specific goal. He had a mission, and nothing could cause him to deviate from that goal. When you get clarity around what your business exists to do for your life and the lives of others, persisting becomes a byproduct. You have everything to gain.

Paul had to leave and turn away from his old mindsets, habits, and life to grow into the leader he was to become. You, too, will have to build a persistent mindset for your story to be the same.

When Paul pursued his goal with singular persistence, it opened the door to an opportunity that would never have been available otherwise. I believe the same is true for you. When you persist in becoming a BLUE Shirt Leader and don't look back, you embody the growth mindset, and it will be worth every moment. There will be trials and difficulties, but as you'll learn from the three Fs below, that's all part of the path to persistence and growth as a leader.

This was my reality when I was developing Right Now Business Coaching. Only a few months into running the business, I realized I needed to build a never-look-back mindset. A verse comes to mind that describes why it is essential for me to have this mindset. In Luke 9:62 (NIV), Jesus says, "No one who puts a hand to the plow and looks back is fit for service in the kingdom of God."

In this verse, Jesus asks His disciples to count the cost before fully committing. You have to count the cost of pursuing your dream and taking the risk if you're going to persist as Paul did. The American basketball player and congressman Bill Bradley said, "Ambition is the path to success. Persistence is the vehicle you arrive in."

Without persistence, every entrepreneur dooms themselves to being one of those statistics shared in chapter 1. But when you commit to becoming the leader you're meant to be, you can achieve amazing things. In the following chapter, you'll learn how to make a vision statement to help you focus and persist in pursuing your goal.

■ Persistence and BLUE Shirt Leadership

In my experience with clients, the comfort of a salaried position, the voices of the naysayers, or the fear of failure prevents them from pursuing their leadership potential. Everyone's reasons for looking back or returning to the easier old habits are different, but you can't go back and at the same time remain persistent in pursuing your goals.

If you want to become a BLUE Shirt Leader, you cannot allow a comfortable salary to be the boat you climb back on. You can't let other people's fears float around your mind and prevent you from taking the necessary actions.

I would like you to spend the next two minutes writing down any distractions, fears, or doubts that cause uncertainty in your mind about your leadership potential. Also, note the people and things that could pull you away from persistence in pursuing your path.

BLUE Shirt Leaders have either adopted or have naturally had a persistent mindset that helps them to make it through challenges, take risks, and learn along the way. The Apostle Paul knew this path all too well. The path to BLUE Shirt Leadership requires you to overcome failure, fatigue, and frustration that can lead to that slide back to the old self.

■ The Three Fs of a Persistent Mindset

Failure

Failure will punch you in the face and make you want to quit. A persistent mindset helps you take your focus off the failure and key into your goals, vision, and values. Being persistent helps you learn from failure and continue taking smart risks to become a BLUE Shirt Leader.

Fatigue

A persistent mindset means you will persist despite fatigue. BLUE Shirt Leaders experience physical, mental, and emotional fatigue, but by choosing proper habits and attitudes they overcome it and persist.

Frustration

The third F is to overcome frustration. As a leader, you discover that frustrations are seemingly endless. Some ways to work through this are by focusing on proper timing, providing clear communication, and sharing your expectations with others. Leaders with a persistent mindset can work through these frustrations and focus on the bigger picture.

Paul had many setbacks on his mission to share the gospel. The same will be true for you and me in our mission to grow as leaders and to leave a lasting impact through our leadership. But as you believe in your vision and persist through the doubts, naysayers, and trials, you will be on your way to BLUE Shirt Leadership.

How do these first three growth mindsets—risk, learner and persistent—work together to help you remodel your leadership house?

■ Risking, Learning, and Persisting for Growth

A risk mindset allows you to learn from your mistakes in real time.

A learner mindset enables you to reflect on these mistakes and apply that learning moving forward.

A persistent mindset gives you the courage to continue learning through mistakes to achieve your goals and vision.

To allow this growth to go beyond your learning and to empower others, you will need to add two more mindsets to this puzzle: abundance and sales mindsets.

When you choose an abundance mindset, you begin to trust the process of self-awareness and accountability within the BLUE Shirt Leadership Framework. You see the potential within yourself and those around you. Your board of advisors becomes of actual value to you.

With an abundance mindset, the risks you take that may not end the way you want are opportunities to learn. As you continue to grow, struggle, fail, and learn, the abundance mindset reminds you to persist through the challenges and victories.

Abundance Mindset

On March 17, 2020, I was about two years into my coaching practice when COVID-19 affected my business. On that day, three companies informed me they were no longer in need of my services because of the sudden shutdowns caused by the pandemic.

Over the three months leading up to March 17, I had set up countless networking calls, gained significant traction in my business with new clients, and filled my funnel for what looked like a strong year ahead. My attitude and energy about my future were fantastic. Business was great!

Losing three clients was devastating. Seventy-five percent of my income was gone. All the hope and energy I had died within a few days after receiving that crushing news. My mood shifted from optimistic and upbeat to discouraged and angry. This loss sent me into a tailspin of "woe is me," and I contemplated closing my business.

After three months of wallowing in self-pity, I still remember sitting at my big executive desk with my head down, freaking out, sweating in the June heat, and realizing my business was failing. Fortunately, I had a breakthrough and a shift in mindset that made all the difference.

While reading David A. Fields' book The Irresistible Consultant's Guide to Winning Clients, I had a moment of clarity. I remember saying aloud, "What am I doing?" It was time to make a change.

I had wallowed in self-pity long enough, and it was time to focus on my clients, adopt an abundance mindset, and get back to what was working.

I investigated my industry to understand what was happening and what was possible. Some staggering statistics about coaching and consulting became a catalyst to stepping up my efforts.

According to research by the ICF (International Coaching Federation), in 2020, coaching industry revenue was $2.849 billion a year worldwide and growing yearly, and consulting revenue was north of $160 billion a year. You could say there's enough money to go around.

Combined with what I learned from Fields' book and those stats, my jaw dropped, and two things became clear. There was (and is) plenty of money to be made in coaching and consulting, regardless of external factors. The failure or success of my business was up to me getting out of my stupid funk. The mindset shift I needed was to have an abundance mindset.

In doing the research and working to recover my business, there were seven lessons I learned that I now use to create and maintain this mindset.

■ 1. Think win-win.

Developing a win-win attitude is the best approach for long-term business success. There have been many networking conversations where I could have quickly burned a bridge by trying to be "salesy" and not thinking win-win. But because I focused on the win-win, often months or even years later, that person referred me to others or became my client. This win-win mentality pays off in spades if you're willing to be patient.

When a recent networking connection signed up for coaching, the win-win approach had proven itself to work and only reinforced what I had learned. Over the past few years, we had connected intermittently, but I had never done the big pitch to her. As a bonus, her husband signed up two weeks later. The win-win game proved to be a great approach. Anytime you focus on adding value, that value will come back to you. Sometimes you won't know when or where, but it will return.

■ 2. Pick your words wisely.

How you say what you say matters. For example, the difference between doing something and getting something is immense. If you tell yourself you "have to" do something, that creates a feeling of obligation and resistance. Shifting to "get to" immediately changes the tone to a much more opportunistic perspective.

When you speak negative words to yourself, your body will respond as if the negative result you're predicting is happening now. Your body and mind will prepare for a battle ahead and approach everything as an attack. By picking your words wisely, the difficulty of the conversation doesn't change, but your attitude and approach do. Shifting to a positive tone allows you to have more clarity and be more effective in your conversation and actions.

Word choice matters in every context of business. The great news is that you completely control what you say and how you say it. Choose words and tones that bring about an attitude of abundance rather than scarcity or limitation. Your words play a vital role in your confidence and growth. An entrepreneur with an abundant mindset will choose and speak words of growth and affirmation.

We all talk to ourselves. You might as well be nice when you do it. An article by Healthline.com states, "Positive self-talk can help you improve your outlook on life. It can also have lasting positive health benefits, including improved well-being and a better quality of life."

■ 3. Be grateful.

According to Harvard Health Publishing, "positive psychology research shows that gratitude is strongly and consistently associated with greater happiness. Gratitude helps people feel more positive emotions, relish experiences, improve their health, deal with adversity, and build strong relationships."

The execution of this idea is simple. Be grateful for what you have and the opportunities you have. You can remain grateful even if you missed opportunities, made mistakes, or things didn't pan out as desired.

A BLUE Shirt Leader learns to be grateful to people for WHO they are and what they accomplished, even if it wasn't what you expected. When you develop an appreciative mindset with team leaders, you help them know you recognize the effort and point out that there are plenty more opportunities. Gratitude opens your mind and heart to what could be. As my dad says, "not what we hoped for, but better than we expected."

■ 4. Surround yourself with people who have an abundance mindset.

Put people with an abundance mindset on your board, on your team, and in your life. Those board members' attitudes will impact and shift yours even if you struggle with this. Seek people with a "default setting" in a life of gratitude. They will positively impact you in more ways than you can count.

"Walk with the dreamers, the believers, the courageous, the cheerful, the planners, the doers, the successful people with their heads in the clouds and their feet on the ground." - Wilfred Peterson.

■ 5. Think big. Then think bigger.

It's way too easy to get too practical in business and to only think about what is right in front of you. Being too detailed or thinking small results from being overwhelmed, busy, or suffering from the burnout many small-business owners experience. There is too much "big" thinking for some business owners, and they need to start putting that thinking to paper.

Whichever style you have, be it thinking too small or too big, use the questions below to review your thoughts about business and leadership. Here are some questions to get you started.

- What would be possible in your leadership if there were no limitations?
- What would you do if you had unlimited resources and couldn't fail?
- What's the cost of NOT pursuing your big ideas?
- What dreams do you have about the future of your business?
- What opportunities would you jump at if your business could make the difference you imagine?

Asking the right questions will serve you well in reaching an abundance mindset.

■ 6. Think like a beginner.

Even if you haven't been a leader (expert) in your field for years and years, you probably know significantly more than your employees, customers, and friends. But an expert mentality gets you in trouble. When you think like a beginner, it can help you look at things from new angles.

With a beginner mindset, you can feel free to ask the "dumb" questions that sometimes bring incredible insights. For example, how often has a child said something that had you saying, "Hmm, that's something I haven't thought about" or "What made you say that?" Children and those with a beginner mindset also have this uncanny ability to summarize things in ways that can be profound and stick with you. A beginner knows there is always more to learn, many ways to grow, and many possibilities.

One approach is to use the "Explain It Like I'm Five" approach. This is an excellent way to determine whether you understand something. It also tends to be a great way to prepare for a presentation on a topic you are an expert on.

One of the best ways to think like a beginner is to turn your big idea into word pictures, explaining what you do through illustrations, analogies, and metaphors. The BLUE Shirt Leadership House is an example of this type of thinking.

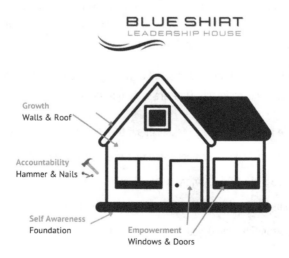

■ Abundance Is Now

The beauty of an abundance mindset is that it sets you up for tremendous business success. When you develop an abundance mindset, you'll find you are already experiencing abundance. At first, this sense of abundance may not show up financially, but it will always come in ideas, opportunities, connections, and much more.

If you imagine the growth mindsets sitting in a minivan, then "abundance" would be the driver and "sales" would be sitting shotgun. I'll share more on this growth SUV later.

You might wonder what happened to my business after I shifted to an abundance mindset during the height of COVID. By the end of the year, I had earned back the clients who had canceled and added several additional clients while doubling my fees. When 2020 wrapped up, my business had grown by 41 percent.

Stop and ask yourself, "How can I shift my thinking today to an abundance mindset?"

Sales Mindset

This book is not about sales, yet a sales mindset is vital to becoming a BLUE Shirt Leader. If you've been in business for years, you know you are always selling.

I ran a pet resort for a few years, and we had what we called "Kennel Hosts" who greeted our guests and their owners. This pet resort sat on forty acres in rural San Luis Obispo, California. The dogs slept in outdoor dog houses 8 feet by 8 feet with a patio of the same size. During the day, they ran freely in one of several off-leash play yards, where they hung out with other "guests" for the day.

The job of the kennel host was to take care of our guests' needs, from water and food to playing and bathing. A radio alert would sound whenever someone crossed a bridge to the resort. This alert meant whoever was closest to the office would drop what they were doing and run (yes, run) to the vehicle parked in front of our office.

Whoever greeted the customer was the person we internally called the "author of first impressions." That host would be responsible for writing the story of that customer's experience (and their dog too). Over time, this story creation built an atmosphere of excitement for both the owner and our furry guests. It also encouraged team members to keep up their enthusiasm and energy for the difficult work.

Because of this "author of first impressions" mindset, do you think the puppy was excited to be there? Do you think this helped sell the owners on the pet resort experience? Of course it did! Why? Because every one of the team members had to maintain this sales mindset so that story could have a win-win ending.

As a result of this "author of first impressions" mindset and many other measures learned and applied along the way, we doubled the pet resort's income in three years—all while our nation endured the 2008 recession.

■ Five Keys to a Sales Mindset

1. Connect with your customer. The best connection happens by asking clarifying questions, listening, and focusing on the needs of the customer. This step is all about building trust. The more you connect with them, the more they trust you and want to do business with you.

2. Focus on pain points. Understand what they are struggling with. What are their concerns? What are they most interested in? You want to address these pain points in your conversation. Then ask what a great outcome would be for them.

3. When selling, make sure there's a plan to address typical objections. Always prepare the sales pitch for common complaints, fears, and objections so you can overcome them quickly and effectively.

4. It's essential to know that you don't have to close the sale on the first pitch! As a salesperson, it's your job to remove their barriers, get them to try your product or service, and get them to see its value. Sometimes, as a leader, you may just need them on board as an early adopter. Knowing their interest and belief in what you're selling can be enough.

5. Finally, you need to be optimistic that the sale will happen (abundance mindset). Believe in yourself and your product, service, or idea. If people can sense an ounce of doubt in your confidence about what you're selling, they will likely lose interest.

As an entrepreneur leader, you know sales isn't only about the products or services you offer. You know there will be times when you need to sell your ideas, vision, and changes. Sales is a mindset that applies to all parts of leadership and business. The sales mindset is a way to engage with others so that you become more influential in whatever you do. The sales mindset will get everyone on board with your ideas and plans when done well.

Besides generating revenue for an organization, maintaining a sales mindset will help leaders get others on board with their ideas. All significant accomplishments result from a successful sale/negotiation. You will always need to sell yourself and your ideas. The sales mindset requires you to have confidence and belief in what you are selling. In the case of leadership, what you're selling is your goals, your values, and yourself. If you don't have confidence in yourself, your leadership will suffer, and so will the confidence of those you lead.

For many entrepreneurs, sales can be a deadly five-letter word. The point is, no matter your relationship with selling, having a strong sales mindset is key to growth. The sales mindset is your primary navigator for business and leadership growth—use it wisely, and you will go far.

Remember the growth vehicle briefly mentioned before? Let's peek through the windows of that SUV of growth. As you drive your business and lean into the growth mindsets, look in the backseat and learn from the *risks* you've taken. Then glance over to their seatmate and be reminded to remain persistent. Sometimes backseat drivers can be helpful.

Trust *abundance*, who is sitting shotgun to help you navigate the rough streets of leadership. Finally, let sales become the driving force of your growth and how you show the world the value of your leadership and business.

When you travel with these mindsets, you're guaranteed growth. Sometimes the terrain will be rough. Other times, you'll be moving along like the road is wide open before you. No matter the road ahead, with these mindsets in your growth SUV you have what you need to keep going and growing!

■ Conclusion

BLUE Shirt Leaders demonstrate they are committed to consistent growth by leaning into these five mindsets.

First, they start by recognizing that, although they might fail along the way to success, failure is not an endpoint but a simple part of the process.

Second, BLUE Shirt Leaders have developed a learner's mindset. The learner's mindset empowers them to receive feedback, learn from mistakes, and seek advice.

Third, BLUE Shirt Leaders learn from the risks they take and continue to lean into their values and goals by staying persistent.

Fourth, BLUE Shirt Leaders know the power of maintaining an abundance mindset. They do this by realizing there is always an abundance of opportunity in the world.

Finally, by bringing all these mindsets together, a BLUE Shirt Leader can make wise decisions and persuasively communicate these decisions with a sales mindset.

Next, you will learn about the habits used by BLUE Shirt Leaders to implement these mindsets.

Chapter 8:

The Growth Habits That Shift Everything

When you see growth in a business, you are really seeing growth in leadership. If you want your business to reach new levels, you must reach new levels in your leadership. To reach new levels as a leader, you must have a growth mindset. A growth mindset differs significantly from a fixed mindset.

People with a fixed mindset believe that their fundamental characteristics, such as intellect or talent, are unchangeable. They also think that talent alone determines success—with no work. The fixed mindset means when you fail once at something, you'll never be able to improve to where others are, so you shouldn't ever try again.

Sounds a bit extreme? Think about the kid that tries a sport once, never to return because they were no good. How about when you tried your hand at a new skill but stumbled? We all have areas where the fixed mindset can creep in.

According to renowned psychologist Carol Dweck, people may be conscious or unaware of their mindsets, yet having a fixed mindset significantly impacts learning achievement, skill acquisition, personal relationships, professional success, and various other aspects of life.

In contrast to the fixed mindset, Dr. Dweck says, "In a growth mindset, people believe that their most basic abilities can be developed through dedication and hard work—brains and talent are just the starting point. This mindset creates a love of learning and resilience essential for great accomplishment."

In this chapter, you will learn five habits to help you lock in the growth mindset.

The **habit of focus** is the catalyst for the growth mindset. The best demonstration of this habit is creating and committing to your vision. This chapter teaches you how to establish a vision and stay committed to it.

You'll learn to **calibrate** your business and leadership to other top performers. When you can measure yourself and your business against high-performing people and firms, you learn and develop while remaining confident. When you calibrate like this, you gain the courage to surpass your self-imposed limitations. In turn, your business will surpass its previous limitations as well.

Next, you'll learn some new perspectives on giving and receiving **feedback**. This lesson is followed by feedback's close cousin, **listening**. Together, these two habits give you the clarity of direction for growth. These habits create a willingness to receive feedback from your board, employees, customers, and coaches while listening deeply and doing something about it.

Finally, the fifth habit is a willingness to **practice** what you've learned and withstand criticism for mistakes and missed opportunities. The practice habit also prepares you for the expected growth to come.

The habits of focus, calibration, feedback, listening, and practice will shift your leadership from a straw house into a building that no big bad wolf can knock down.

■ How's Your Leadership House?

At the beginning of this book, I used a metaphor for your leadership called the BLUE Shirt Leadership House. This metaphor describes self-awareness as the foundation, accountability as the nails, growth as the walls and roof, and empowerment as the windows and doors. The advantage of using these leadership pillars is that there isn't a natural conclusion or a completion point.

Leaning on the growth pillar means that sometimes you have to remodel, tear down, and even blow the roof off what you thought was possible in your leadership and business. When you genuinely embody the mindsets and habits in this book, the only option is to remodel!

The five growth habits of focus, calibration, feedback, listening, and practice may seem like an odd list of habits to develop one's leadership, but as you read on you'll see why these habits are vital to becoming the leader you're meant to be.

The Focus Habit

John D. Rockefeller said, "Singleness of purpose is one of the chief essentials for success in life, no matter what may be one's aim."

What is your focus? What are you REALLY trying to accomplish? My focus (or the vision for my business) is to empower thousands of leaders to take control of their mindsets and habits to become the leaders they are meant to be.

Within this vision, people can find themselves mentally, emotionally, physically, and spiritually free to accomplish what God has planned for them. But when you are overwhelmed, under-confident, and working/living without clarity of mind or habits, none of this will happen.

There are specific things you are designed to achieve, but you can get in your own way! The BLUE Shirt Leadership Framework unlocks the chains that bind you to mediocrity, limited belief, and lack of freedom to do what you are meant to.

But to get there, you must have a growth mindset. You must have a vision.

You must have a clear and present focus that drives you.

For Rockefeller, his focus was the relentless pursuit of wealth. For Michael Jordan and Kobe Bryant, it was the drive to be the best that ever played the game of basketball. Martin Luther King Jr. gave his utmost for God.

Now think back to the stories you've read about so far: The story of the boy in the river. Colonel Sanders developing a successful franchise at an age when most people are considering retirement. Kobe on the basketball court while Jay Williams watches in awe. The Apostle Paul enduring through trial and persecution. Even that unfortunate butterfly the little girl was trying to help. They all demonstrate the habit of focus.

How well you focus will depend on your commitment to and communication of your vision. Are you willing to put the work in and focus like the people did in the examples shared throughout this book?

■ Discover Your Vision

Without vision, there is no horizon for a leader to move toward. Proverbs 29:18 (KJV) says, "Where there is no vision, the people perish." Without vision, there is no lighthouse for a leader's followers to find when things get hazy.

Staying focused on your vision is what lights up your leadership house. It is like the power of the building. Without it, people are groping around in the dark, bumping into things, and making a horrible mess.

Do you know anyone who leads without a clear vision? How is their business performing? How are their employees performing? The metaphor is obvious. You are blind without a vision; without vision, those you influence are unable to follow you.

■ A Journey from California to Washington

In 2014, my family and I moved from San Luis Obispo, California, to Bellingham, Washington. It took about six months for us to decide on the destination. It was one of the most challenging decisions of our lives.

We moved from beautiful, sunny California weather, beaches, surfing, ministry, and friends to where my wife's family was in Bellingham, Washington. I'm fortunate to have a great relationship with my family and in-laws. My wife, Kari, can say the same. So, the decision was heart-wrenching because it felt like we were choosing one family over the other.

Things were very unclear for a few months. I'd imagined myself joining the family business and owning an orange farm. But that vision wasn't the right fit for my own family. Yet, the Pacific Northwest was such an unknown.

My problem was that I didn't have a clear vision of where I should go or where to lead my family. Eventually, we moved to Bellingham with the vision to impact people there as we had in San Luis Obispo.

This vision was a bold step for us but served as the catalyst that moved us forward. This simple focus ultimately helped start what has become Right Now Business Coaching and get this book into your hands. I'm still marching along to the call of this vision with focus.

■ Busyness and Hazy Windows

You probably get so busy just doing the day-to-day that you often forget to look up and see where you're heading. If you've ever felt like you are working by default or creating what others want from you instead of what you want, then developing the habit of focus will change your leadership, business, and life.

Unfortunately, too many business owners are on autopilot, just making it through the day. However, when your vision stays focused, it's like looking through a clean windshield, windows, and mirrors in your growth SUV, as described in the previous chapter.

You can see the future through the windshield, the present through the side windows, and the past in the mirrors. In a car, it's pretty apparent when the windows and mirrors get foggy or dirty. You can't see where you are going or what is happening.

And when that happens, it spells danger. Maintaining the habit of focus helps you see the terrain around you and clarify direction.

I remember lying awake at night with tears running down my face and dripping onto my pillow. We were six months into living in Washington, and I was struggling with losing what I'd had in California. I knew it was okay to mourn what I had lost, but it took another year to recognize what the problem was about that night. It wasn't the tears. Those tears were healthy and good.

The problem was that I had my head down, and my focus was no longer on my future. If I did look up, it was into the rearview mirrors. When I could finally look through the windshield, it was hazy. I could not see where I was going or where I was taking my family. It was unclear, and we could have been quickly heading into a brick wall.

You've been there before, haven't you? You lose focus, and the next thing you know you're off the road and making a mess. If you're off track, imagine its impact on those you lead! You wake up and realize that the original path you set, or your selected plan, has been forgotten or lost.

Think about a road trip you've taken with friends or family. If you think about it, arriving at the destination wasn't the best part, was it? Sure, it was fun, but the best parts of the trip were the conversations in the car, the laughter at the restaurant, and the adventures you went on as you traveled. The unexpected or spontaneous moments are usually the best.

Next time you get into your car, where are you focused most of the time? Are you looking in your mirrors, through your side windows, or out the windshield? Looking through these "windows" at times is important, but focusing on the road is essential.

This section will help you develop a vision to give you the focus you need. A vision statement needs your past, present, and future pieces to be effective. A clear vision statement is your true north for your leadership future.

With a powerful vision statement, you will know what to move toward and what to steer away from. You'll know whom to spend time with and whom to avoid. When you're not in step with your vision, you will know it. When you are in harmony with your vision, you'll know it too!

Couple this clear vision statement with all the mindsets and habits you've read about, and you're guaranteed a fantastic journey as you focus on your vision!

■ A Vision Statement Locks In Your Growth Mindset

When you know where you want to go, you'll be surprised at how many doors will suddenly open to you. Lacking vision is like walking around in the dark. Your path won't be straight. You'll meander back and forth and wonder why you haven't found a clear direction.

Your vision statement is a lighthouse for you and those you lead. When you aren't sure where you need to go, focus on your vision statement as your guide. Let the lighthouse guide your way when failures, fatigue, and frustrations wear on you. Your actions, work, and relationships will have a guiding light to focus on. You'll have more clarity about what to do. Your vision will guide you forward even when things seem dark and the path is hazy.

Unfortunately, many people don't have a vision statement because it is challenging to create. But with the work you've done before this, you should have great clarity on the crucial elements you need to make your vision statement.

It is essential to recognize that a vision statement doesn't have to be perfect and can be modified. Life changes. Business changes. But the heart of your vision statement won't change much.

However, your vision statement needs to come from you and from a place that ties to your values, strengths, and the future. It is part of your leadership tool kit and helps guide your life and grow your influence. It's important to recognize that developing your first vision statement may take you more than a weekend or longer to feel fully committed. That's okay. It took me six months to get a vague idea of what mine could be.

■ Developing Your Vision Statement

Step 1: Schedule a block of time (at least two to three hours) to get started. Leading up to this block of time, make sure to have your notes app or a notepad ready throughout the day and week to jot down ideas that come to mind.

Start by responding to the following questions:

- What will you lose if you stay safe, stay here, and don't chase your dreams?
- Imagine you are eighty years old and looking back at your life. Which dream from your list would cause you the greatest regret if you had NOT pursued it?
- Imagine three years have gone by and they were the best three years of your life. What were the top one to three things you accomplished that have given you a tremendous sense of pride, success, and happiness?
- If in three years you are disappointed with your results, why will that be? (Let's be honest, we always know why we'll fail at something).
- What's something you could do that you've never done before that might make all the difference?

Step 2: Consider the environment. For some, it may be helpful to do this in a different context or take a slightly different approach than sitting at a desk and brainstorming.

- Get into nature to help you think more clearly and be inspired.
- Visit your local library and borrow a quiet conference room.
- Find a river, waterfall, or beach where you can spend time in reflection.
- Meditate or pray about your vision statement.
- Use a whiteboard or flip chart to brainstorm habits, goals, and dreams.
- Work with a coach or someone else and share the experience.

Once you determine your approach, move to Step 3.

Step 3: Slow down, take a breath, and pause for a moment. Start working on your vision statement by taking time to pray/meditate/reflect on your future.

What is the optimistic and inspiring picture that you see?

Step 4: Create a few drafts using a "To..., so that..." or "I will..., so that..." model. Try incorporating your responses and ideas into one or two powerful and memorable statements.

For example:

- I will help thousands of business owners shift their mindsets and habits so they can become the leaders they are meant to be.
- To provide a caring, friendly, and fun atmosphere to our furry guests so their owners can enjoy worry-free vacations and workdays away from their dogs.

These statements do not have to be perfect the first time. You can revisit them several times before choosing the one that fits best.

Step 5: Take some time throughout the next few weeks to repeat your vision statements aloud, share them with friends, or be bold and share them with a stranger at a coffee shop.

During this reflective time, you may create a few more drafts. The extra time to reflect will help you get a feel for your vision and how they fit you and allow you to gain more clarity. The point of using this extra time is to connect deeply with the vision statement so that it easily rolls off your tongue and rattles around in your head.

Once the statement is in place, the habit of focusing on this vision will change everything. In this next section, you will learn to consider possibilities like never before.

The Calibration Habit

I'm a huge NBA fan. There's a debate around who is the GOAT (Greatest of All Time) in the basketball world. Even if you're not a basketball fan, you'll recognize these names: Michael Jordan, Kobe Bryant, and LeBron James.

With Michael Jordan's career starting earlier than Kobe and LeBron's, the comparison is usually to Michael Jordan. Most people don't know whom Michael Jordan modeled his game after. Jordan's basketball hero was Walter Davis, a six-time all-star who played fifteen years in the NBA. Davis also went to North Carolina, where Jordan chose to play in college.

Kobe and LeBron mention they modeled portions of their game after Jordan's and put him as the calibration standard.

Ultimately, each of these players believes they are the greatest. They've all said it in interviews! But the point is not who is the basketball GOAT. The fact is, each of these players has modeled and calibrated their game after other excellent examples.

In business leadership, you need to do the same. The habit of calibrating is vital for your business and leadership to grow. I have chosen this word precisely because it's not about copying or comparing in the usual way.

The calibration habit helps you to measure your performance (or intended performance) with great leaders you'd like to model your leadership after.

The definition of calibrate is instructive here. It includes "to correlate the readings of (an instrument) with those of a standard to check the instrument's accuracy. To take external factors into account or to allow comparison with other data, and to carefully assess, set, or adjust (something abstract)."

When you calibrate, you will correlate what is happening in your business and leadership to an external standard. This gives you an objective example to measure against. If a measuring cup weren't always calibrated to eight ounces, you would have some messed-up brownies, which is unacceptable.

When you calibrate, you take external factors associated with your business into account and compare these to your competitors or other data to help you make decisions. Finally, calibration allows you to assess, reset, and adjust your business and leadership.

Calibrating to other leaders and businesses allows you to track growth in measurable and more abstract areas of your leadership and business. The calibration habit unlocks so much new awareness that it's genuinely incredible.

How do you implement this habit? It begins with research. Research who are the most outstanding leaders in your niche market. Also, find out the most successful businesses in your niche market.

The goal isn't to copy and compare but to measure yourself and your business against these "standards" to know where you stand. Don't get into a comparison trap; rather, use this information as an opportunity to learn and grow.

Some suggestions to help you with this research include:

- Read the biographies of great leaders.
- Look at your competitors' reviews to see why their customers love them (or hate them).
- Implement and enhance processes that are like other businesses in your market.
- Learn what great leaders in your industry read, write, and talk about.
- Interact with thought leaders inside and outside your niche.
- Monitor the sales, marketing, and branding of those in your niche.

This list can go on, but for now, take some time to write which of these you want to act on. Keep in mind that the habit of calibration requires consistent effort. Once you know the key areas to focus on, measure, and document your progress, let the habit of calibration guide your actions.

You're on to something when you act like the leaders in the biographies you choose to read. You're growing when you enhance or innovate based on the processes your competitors use. When your competitor's marketing strategy sparks a better idea for your business, you've got this habit down.

Don't apply this habit to become like everyone else in your market. Instead, when you have the pulse of what is happening in your niche and how people lead within the niche, you will differentiate yourself and your business and blow the competition away.

In the next section, we look at a close cousin to calibration: feedback—the giving and receiving of internal and external feedback on your business and leadership.

The Feedback Habit

From 2006 to 2014, almost every week, I had lunch with the president of the Alpha Academy. Jack and I would meet at one of about half a dozen restaurants in the San Luis Obispo area. My favorite restaurant to visit was Tahoe Joe's. I love their Bacon Bleu Burger.

I had a few different roles within the non-profit organization during this time. For three and a half years, I managed the Thousand Hills Pet Resort (which provided the funding for the non-profit Alpha Academy). For the final four years, I was the director of Alpha Academy, where Jack was the president.

During my meetings with Jack, we would discuss the state of the pet resort or Alpha Academy. These lunches were typically ninety minutes long, and we covered business strategy, employee development, finances, and various other topics.

But there was another topic we consistently covered that helped my leadership growth: me. We talked about what I was doing well, where help was needed, and changes to make. We followed the three fundamental questions formula we asked every Alpha Academy student.

Those questions are:

- Where am I?
- Where do I want to go?
- How do I get there?

These three questions helped form the foundation of the leader I am today. These three questions are the questions that provide you with the feedback you need to develop as a leader. If you have people internally and externally asking these questions in some form, you will grow. The feedback is powerful.

When a friend of mine pointed out that I don't take enough risks, he asked, "Where are you with risk-taking?" This led to asking the following two questions from the list above. Where do I want to be with risk-taking? How am I going to get there?

Feedback can be both internal and external. It is received and given. For input feedback to matter, you must accept it. Sometimes this is hard to do when you aren't in the right place mentally, and sometimes the other person doesn't deliver the feedback well. Proverbs 1:5 (NKJV) addresses both types of feedback: "A wise man will hear and increase in learning. And a man of understanding will acquire wise counsel."

Sometimes people share feedback that tells you where you are. Other times, you get feedback on where they wish you could be. And sometimes people give feedback telling you how to get to a specific place.

When you get or give feedback, use the three questions listed above to help you filter what you hear or share. The answers to these questions can help you take a step back, gain a better perspective, and get the most from the conversation. You can evaluate the message objectively.

Back to the risk feedback conversation. Recently, a friend gave me some harsh feedback at a coffee shop. He told me I don't take enough risks. He said I'm playing it safe. When filtered through the questions Where am I? and Where do I want to go? his feedback turned into powerful insight.

Immediately, I realized I wasn't where I wanted to be with some physical goals and risks I wanted to take. I also realized I wasn't where I wanted to be financially. This conversation turned into a climb to the top of Mt. Shasta and a fee shift in my business. Feedback works when filtered correctly.

Filtering feedback through these three questions can become a habit when you create weekly accountability, as mentioned in chapter 6.

My habit of active accountability every week has continued since leaving the Alpha Academy in California. Currently, I have Right Now Mastermind meetings with other business owners. These meetings are feedback sessions and help each of us in many ways.

The Mastermind meetings provide a context for accountability and growth in business. In the meetings, we all share what's REALLY going on. We share struggles, victories, hopes, and mistakes, and sometimes just complain. The back-and-forth nature of these conversations has allowed me to grow in remarkable ways.

We've met for coffee, walks, hikes, pickleball, racquetball, and other things. However, feedback is always the backbone of our meetings.

In your business, carve out time to meet with your employees so you can give and receive feedback. The meetings can be lunches like I had with Jack or like my ten-minute Tuesdays with Phil (I'll share this later).

Ideally, you would have a combination of these meetings. You can meet for coffee, meet over lunch, or drop by and chat. this time serves as an opportunity for everyone to give and receive feedback. Maybe nothing will change in a day, but significant changes occur when you create a weekly pattern of these interactions.

The feedback habit allows you to consistently give and receive input about your leadership from all stakeholders. Feedback helps you to stay focused on your vision, be challenged to grow, and put into practice what you hear. Feedback brings perspective. It's like a mountaintop view of what is going on in your leadership and business.

Combining the tool of feedback with the habit of focus can help you stay on target with what you are trying to achieve through your business. Feedback is a great tool to do that. Calibrating to the performance of great leaders and businesses inside and out of your industry is also a powerful feedback mechanism.

As you progress, the feedback you receive needs to be accepted and turned into actions you can practice. But before we get to the practice habit, let's look at the often-forgotten leadership habit of listening.

The Listening Habit

As Larry King once said, "I remind myself every morning: Nothing I say this day will teach me anything. So, if I'm going to learn, I must do it by listening."

You create a better business environment and become a better leader when you listen. When you choose to listen to others, they will choose to listen to you. And when you listen, you validate the worth of the other.

When I worked at Alpha Academy, the men's mentoring program, I instituted ten-minute Tuesdays. At the time, there were three students in the program. We met one-on-one weekly in private to chat about what was happening in their lives.

The intention was to learn how their week went and discuss their concerns or anything else on their minds. After successful meetings with the other two students, it was Phil's turn. Phil was not much of a talker and trusted almost no one.

I thought I was prepared for the first meeting with Phil as we sat down side-by-side, about four feet from one another. I looked over and asked, "Hey, Phil, how's it going?" He stared straight ahead at the closet door directly in front of us.

After a few moments, I asked again. Still no response. A few moments passed. I asked again how things were. Still no response. I had set a timer, and when I looked down I saw we still had over eight minutes to go. Determined to honor the idea and let it play out, we sat there in silence for the remaining eight minutes.

As soon as the time was up, Phil got up and walked out.

Another week came and went. It was again time to meet with Phil. We had exchanged only a few words throughout the week, and they weren't always pleasant. I figured this meeting was going to be rough. It started the same: "Hey, Phil, how's it going?" followed by ten minutes of silence.

When the next week rolled around, I was ready to give up on the whole idea of ten-minute Tuesdays. The meeting started the same way. "Hey, Phil, how's it going?" After several seconds, I was ready to let him know he could leave. As Phil stared at the wall, he said, "Fine." I was shocked. I wasn't exactly sure what to do next.

After getting over the shock, we had a somewhat stilted conversation about his day and the program. He had opened up, and that was a start. This meeting would begin a genuine relationship in which Phil eventually learned to trust me. When I bumped into him in town a couple of years later, he ran up and gave me a big hug.

When was the last time you patiently and silently listened to those you lead? Think about the last conversation you had. How about a recent team meeting? Did your employees or clients perceive you as a listener? How do you think that impacts your leadership?

BLUE Shirt Leaders recognize the power of listening and silence. They have learned the WISER way to listen. They understand that listening is a skill. We try to understand, empathize with, and persuade people as we speak and listen.

In Stephen R. Covey's fantastic book *The 7 Habits of Highly Effective People,* the fifth habit is "Seek First to Understand Then Be Understood." If you have a listener's mindset, you need to seek first to understand, then to be understood. Couple this with the platinum habit, and you are well on your way to great listening.

When Phil and I sat together, I could have lectured him about opening up and at least saying something; but for some reason, I waited and sat in silence. I (uncomfortably) chose to remain silent and prepared to listen. This waiting in silence turned into trust, and he finally felt heard. I gave him the space so I could understand him and he could feel understood.

Before we move to the practice habit, I want to share a practical way to sharpen your listening skills.

■ The WISER Way to Listen

John said to his wife, "You're the engineer of a train. There are twenty-two people on board. At the first stop, three passengers get off, and eight get on. At the next stop, ten passengers get off, and three get on. What is the name of the engineer?"

Scowling, John's wife said, "How should I know?" John looked at her and said, "See, you don't listen! I said at the beginning, you're the engineer of a train."

This silly story illustrates a simple point. Many people don't listen. Even when we are "listening" to those closest to us, we have difficulty hearing what they say. Let's first get some facts out there, then move on to some practical ways to improve your listening skills:

- ➲ We talk at a rate of 125 words per minute but can <u>comprehend</u> 400 words per minute.
- ➲ Less than 2 percent of people have had any formal <u>education</u> on how to listen.
- ➲ Images reside in your long-term memory, whereas words live in your short-term memory.

Another interesting fact is that, while you can listen and comprehend up to 400 words per minute, you would still have over 65 percent of your ability to listen. Excess brain power makes it challenging to pay attention at times. If you've ever found yourself eavesdropping on a friend's conversation while having one of your own, you've engaged that extra 65 percent.

The other reality many people face is not having formal training in how to listen. If you think about it, there aren't too many experts in any field who have achieved success without some type of formal training. Listening is no exception.

The third fact I provided above about listening relates imagery with comprehension. Words can make an impression and may even elicit an emotional response, but long-term memory is activated when you pair them with related imagery. If you want to listen well or keep people's attention, try using as many senses as possible.

■ Three Verses to Help You Be a Better Listener

The Bible serves as one of the best sources of instruction for life. Regarding listening, it includes no fewer than seventy-three verses. Here are three verses that help us listen—or, as *Merriam-Webster's Dictionary* says, "give one's attention to a sound"—better:

1. In James 1:19–20 (NASB), we learn to wait before we speak. James says, "My dear brothers and sisters, take note of this: Everyone should be quick to listen, slow to speak and slow to become angry, because human anger does not produce the righteousness that God desires." So much of the time we speak too quickly and under false assumptions. Instead let's be quick to listen, not quick to speak.

2. In Luke 2:46 (NASB) we read, "Then, after three days they found Him [Jesus] in the temple, sitting in the midst of the teachers, both listening to them and asking them questions." At a very young age, Jesus was adept at engaging by listening and asking questions. Jesus teaches us here to listen intently and to ask great questions. He sat among the experts in their field and learned a great deal from them. In the next verse, we discover that even as a young boy, Jesus had great insight to offer as well. Sometimes even the teacher needs to listen.

3. Proverbs 3:1–2 (NIV) says, "My child, remember my teachings and instructions and obey them completely. They will help you live a long and prosperous life." The writer of this proverb is showing us the value of reviewing and remembering the things we are told.

■ Wait for Your Turn

Waiting while someone is speaking can be as hard as sitting in silence. One tool to help you wait patiently is this: Assume the person talking doesn't want to hear what you have to say. Most of the time, if someone wants your input, they will ask for it. A great mnemonic device here is W.A.I.T.: Why Am I Talking? However, waiting to talk differs from asking questions or clarifying meaning by summarizing what was said.

The second part of "wait your turn" is to be okay with a eight seconds of silence. In other words, as you listen to someone, keep a timer in your head that allows for an eight-second pause in dialogue before you dive in with something to say. This gives the person you're conversing with time to think and get their thoughts out without interruption.

■ Imagine Their Story

A good story transports you to a different place. Your mind is engaged beyond the words, and you begin to "see and feel" the story. You begin to experience the story's context more deeply, seeing, touching, hearing, tasting, and smelling the story being told.

You can use your imagination when you listen to others, even if the story is simple. A friend tells you about a breakup they are going through. Imagine yourself in the room where they had the tough conversation. Imagine the attitudes and words. Insert yourself into the emotions of the context. Put yourself in his/her shoes as you listen.

If they struggle to tell engaging stories, ask questions that draw on the imagination, such as, "What did it sound like? What did you see? How did you feel?"

■ Summarize What You've Heard

When you put yourself in the speaker's shoes and have a clear image and understanding of the message, you can summarize what you have heard. Summarizing is arguably the best first response to what someone has said. It clarifies and shows you caught the main points. More importantly, it shows you care. And if you got it wrong, that gives the speaker a chance to clarify and keep everyone on the same page.

The summary doesn't have to be perfect or hit on every point. It needs to highlight what matters in the conversation's context and situation. When we do this, we engage the speaker and the situation. The key to summaries is making sure you share when it makes sense. Wait until the speaker is done with what they have to say, then respond with, "What I hear you saying is ...."

■ Engage the Speaker

There are many ways to engage someone who is speaking. Many of these engagements don't require words. You can nod or shake your head, frown, smile, laugh, or take notes. Eye contact is the best form of engagement. Engaging without words allows the person speaking to feel comfortable and know they are being listened to. It also provides intermittent feedback to ensure you're on the same page.

With that said, listening to someone does not exclude asking questions. Sometimes asking questions is the most effective way to engage the speaker and listen to their story (more on this in chapter 9).

When each of these first four steps of WISER listening is used correctly, the final step ensures you have genuinely listened and can retain what you were told.

■ Review the Conversation

Research has shown that taking notes and reflecting on conversations or content within ten minutes will help you recall the information. This will help lock the information into your long-term memory. If you aren't reviewing the information you've heard or aren't able to recall the information, are you really listening?

Spend some time after key conversations to think about what was said and the meaning behind what was said. Preferably this would be done a few minutes after the discussion, but you can also review key conversations at the end of the day.

■ The WISER Way to Listen

Listening requires effort, but the effort will pay off in unique ways. From deeper relationships to better business negotiations, listening intently and responding slowly is worth the work.

- Wait for permission to speak and be okay with silence.
- Imagine their story. Use all your senses.
- Summarize what has been said when appropriate.
- Engage by asking questions, taking notes, making noises, and keeping eye contact.
- Review what you heard later that day to learn from the conversation and reflect on the meaning of what was said.

Who is the best listener in your life? What makes them a great listener?

Before you continue reading, stop and think about the ten-minute Tuesday story. If you're not already considering starting your ten-minute Tuesday with those you lead (family included), I challenge you to start right here and now.

What would ten minutes of your undivided attention do for your employees? These ten-minute meetings change businesses and lives. Employees want to know that you trust and believe in them. They know you care when you are purposeful in listening, even for this short amount of time.

With the last habit of the chapter, we turn to sports again. Let's talk about the habit of practice.

The Practice Habit

On February 4, 2007, the Indianapolis Colts beat the Chicago Bears 29–17 in Super Bowl XLI. The teams played the game in cold and rainy conditions. There were eight turnovers between the teams, five of them being fumbles. Bears quarterback Rex Grossman had two fumbles himself.

For the Colts, it was an ugly game, but they won. Most NFL fans didn't notice a hidden component to the game: the constant exchange of Jeff Saturday hiking the ball to Peyton Manning.

As ugly as the game was, there was not a single fumble or bobbled snap between Jeff and Peyton throughout the entire game. Had there been just one, it could have had devastating consequences for the Colts. If you watch the highlights, many players drop perfectly placed passes or fumble the ball. But Jeff and Peyton were perfect.

So how was it possible for Peyton Manning and Jeff Saturday to have so many successful exchanges? One word: practice.

Manning and Saturday would take snaps before practice every day. Of course, they would take snaps during training as well. But every center/quarterback combination does this. What was unique for them was that they would do what Peyton Manning called the wet-ball drill. Peyton had been doing this since his college days in Tennessee.

The wet-ball drill was one of those annoying Peyton Manning preparations. They'd dunk footballs in five-gallon buckets, and the ball would get heavy, wet, and hard to handle. From this practice, Jeff would get wet and annoyed while Peyton was trying to figure out how to hold the wet ball and adjust his grip.

Regardless of the annoyance, this practice habit helped the Colts win Superbowl XLI.

■ Practice in Business

No matter what market your business is in, there are many skills that you can practice. Here are some ideas to help get you thinking of your own wet-ball drills.

Practice your elevator pitch (your thirty-second sales pitch to a prospect). Periodically, also revisit your elevator pitch and share it with people. In fact, taking part in some networking groups will give you the opportunity to share it weekly.

B.L.U.E Shirt Leadership Framework

Practice your sales presentations. Before you go into a sales conversation, take the time to act out the presentation in your mind. Imagine the successful experience in detail and with a lot of energy and enthusiasm. Specifically, get comfortable asking for the sale and the fee you anticipate.

Practice your PowerPoint presentations. If you work in a business where you must present to others, you know the importance of reviewing the quality of your presentation and practicing. Practicing what you say to your team once or twice can improve your message. As you practice this, here are some things to consider:

- What do I want my presentation to convey?
- Imagine what it would look like for you to have a successful presentation. What will the audience experience?

Practice difficult conversations. Run through your mind several times the difficult conversations you need to have. It may also be helpful to share what you intend to say with a colleague. To help you think about these conversations, review the following items.

- If they say x, I will respond and say...
- At the end of the conversation, how do I want the person to feel: Heard? Encouraged?
- What is the result I'm looking for?

Practice saying no. Get comfortable saying no. Practice this habit by not responding to emails and other small requests to improve your ability to say no to the bigger things.

Practice the Socratic Method. Practice turning employee questions back around on them. Take a few mental steps back and ask open-ended questions to get them thinking for themselves. You don't need to think for them (more on this in the next chapter).

Practice saying yes to ideas. While saying no is something small business owners need to improve, many small business owners also struggle to accept change. Practice embracing minor changes. Practice considering these things and the disruption that you didn't expect or an idea that doesn't exactly fit.

Practice taking breaks in your day. Give yourself time and space in your day to rest and allow your mind to perform at its best. Review the transition moments section in chapter 4 for more ideas on taking breaks.

Finally, and possibly most importantly, a great exercise to practice is writing in the present tense what you would like to see happen in 250 words or less and how it makes you feel. For example, you could write the following:

This week, the work on the project went well and I have three new projects lined up. My conversation with Amy went well, and we are on the same page again. I've been able to help Charles understand that my plate is full and said no to his requests. I've been feeling great about taking short breaks in my day. These breaks are helping me stay focused, and I feel like I'm a lot more productive and leading the team well.

In the example above, you are anticipating a successful week and are imagining the feelings of this success before it happens. This practice creates cognitive dissonance in your unconscious from your conscious. This dissonance makes your unconscious go to work to make this imagined future a reality.

When you use this final practice, picturing desired future scenarios in your mind's eye will help you adjust your current actions, often resulting in the desired future.

Before you read the next section, write the three to five things you need to practice, then in 250 words or less, describe your success with adopting these practices and how that success will make you feel.

■ A Bundle of Habits

The way you live your life and complete your workdays reflects your habits. Thinking about it for a moment, your leadership is just a bundle of habits. As you read about the habits in this book, you can choose to improve on the proper habits and drop the weak or bad ones.

If you are going to reach the leadership level that you want, you must eliminate habits that distract you from your goals, emphasize your weaknesses, or are simply bad for you. When you deepen your self-awareness and establish exceptional accountability in your life and business, you will unravel the bundle of habits that make up your day-to-day leadership choices. The set of habits described in this book will help you build good habits and eliminate bad ones more quickly than you may have thought possible.

At the end of the book is a simple 10-day plan. These chapters will help you implement the mindsets and habits of a BLUE Shirt Leader. Next, we will shift from primarily self-focused areas of BLUE Shirt Leadership to the others-focused pillar, empowerment.

Ready to supercharge your results with the BLUE Shirt Leadership Framework? Don't wait! Apply now for a consultation with Kyle Gillette and receive personalized guidance to fast-track your success. Take the first step towards transformative leadership.

SCAN HERE

Chapter 9:

Empowerment Mindsets

In 2015, CEO Dan Price raised the salary of everyone at Gravity Payments to a base salary of $70,000 per year. He also shrunk his salary from $1 million down to $70,000. Many in the organization saw him as a hero, and others predicted this bold move would fail.

With the average American CEO salary 320 times greater than their entry-level employees, what Dan Price did was a bold and risky move. He could bankrupt his business and be ostracized by fellow CEOs, or it could all work and transform the company and the employees' lives in bold new ways.

Five years into Gravity Payments' bold experiment, COVID hit. The business took a 55 percent loss, which put Dan and his company within four months of failing. But they didn't; they bounced back and survived.

How did they do this when businesses were shutting down and filing bankruptcy right and left?

When the employees learned of the company's possible future, they voluntarily took pay cuts to help the business survive. The business survived. In fact, by the third quarter of 2021, the company's revenue tripled partly because the employees' temporary pay cuts had provided the cash flow needed to get back on track.

What's impressive is that after the company recovered, Dan Price paid back all his employees for the cuts they'd taken, and even provided many with raises! The story doesn't end here.

His employees wanted to thank the CEO for his hard work, generosity, and kindness. So collectively, all the employees decided to chip in and bought him a Tesla. Upon receiving the generous gift, Dan was speechless.

He told others what had happened: "My employees have done way more for me than I could ever do for them. The fact that they wanted to get me such an unreal, amazing gift is pretty special. I don't know if I can put it into words how this makes me feel."

Whether you agree with Dan's approach to paying his employees and his compensation, one thing is undeniably clear: Dan and his employees are fiercely loyal and genuinely care about each other. What we see here is a genuine demonstration of uncommon kindness.

Dan Price tweeted on April 12, 2021: "6 years ago today, I raised my company's min wage to $70k. Fox News called me a socialist whose employees would be on bread lines. Since then, our revenue has tripled, we're a Harvard Business School case study & our employees had a 10x boom in homes bought. — Always invest in people."

Dan Price and his employees exemplify the empowerment pillar of the BLUE Shirt Leadership Framework and the mindset of kindness. BLUE Shirt Leaders approach their relationships both inside and outside of work with uncommon kindness.

Dan said it best in his tweet, "Always invest in people." That's what the empowerment pillar is all about: investing in your people first.

Kindness Mindset

In many ways, kindness is like the warmth of your leadership house.

My aunt and uncle lived two orange groves (a three-minute walk) away when I was a kid. Every time I was in their home, I felt comfortable and cared for and had no desire to leave. It was never a place that I just went to get something and go. Their home's inherent warmth and kindness made me want to stay and settle in.

Their house was clean and comfortable. My aunt would always offer a snack or drink whenever I stopped in. She and my uncle always greeted me with a smile and a hug. There was a genuine feeling of being welcomed in their home.

As you lead, consider what kindness you bring to those you lead. How welcoming are you in your leadership and business? Is your leadership inviting and warm like my aunt and uncle's house, or does it feel aloof and cold?

Supportive leaders will find this kindness mindset easy, but this is not to say you can't be a hard-nosed, driven leader and still be kind. To be kind, you don't have to pay everyone $70,000 as a starting wage. There are hundreds of things you can do to make your leadership house feel warm, welcoming, and kind.

Why does the kindness mindset work? In my previous job as an HR manager, for over two-and-a-half years I consistently interacted with the executive team members. Whether it was fair or not, the two executives that demonstrated kindness and attention got my absolute best.

I did work for the third executive, but the quality of my service to him wasn't where it could have been. It was hard to tell what he wanted because he failed to connect with me and didn't exhibit kindness.

When you reflect on your experiences, you may have behaved this way, too. I bet if you look at your current or past situations, you can think of a time when you might have shown a lack of kindness. How did that employee perform for you?

Kindness is like a turbo boost for empowering employees to perform well. If better quality work and attention to detail are your goals, why not extend a little kindness? As parents we can't spank kids into performing better, nor can we bully our team members into better work performance. Kindness is the key.

When companies focus on kindness, they see tangible results. For example:

- Organizations that focused on a culture of kindness realized 901 percent stock price growth over eleven years compared to 74 percent for those that didn't.

- Two major quick service food industry companies focused on kindness had 14 percent and 24 percent annual turnover rates—in stark contrast to the rest of the industry, which averages a 170 percent turnover rate.

- According to a study by McKinsey, 70 percent of the buying experience is based on kindness .

- Southwest Airlines has delivered forty-six years of profitability and has had zero layoffs and zero wage decreases, with an average turnover of only 3 percent. Why? Because the company puts kindness to employees and customers at the heart of the business.

Kindness costs very little but pays great dividends.

S. Truett Cathy, founder of Chick-fil-A.

Okay, so I am sure by now you get it. There is a tremendous benefit to showing kindness. So how can you raise your kindness key performance indicator? Although there are many ways to show kindness, start by thinking from the position of caring, friendly, and fun. Here are a few kindnesses shifts you can start today:

1. Smile. It costs nothing but is priceless.

2. Think more about we, not me. Share in the credit but own the mistakes.

3. Give some of your time, resources, or love every day.

4. Get out from behind the desk or the steering wheel and go out of your way to connect with someone.

5. Have fun and laugh during meetings, lunches, and challenging times.

6. Create a kinder return policy or cancellation policy.

7. Be flexible. There are circumstances and situations where not being so stiff makes sense.

8. Empower your team to be kind by giving them the freedom to do nice things on behalf of your business. Allow them to provide a discount or offer a gift to loyal customers, or supply your employees with gift cards to share.

9. Make it a policy to walk around catching people doing something good. Then personally thank them for their work.

10. Focus on your people and customers more than on your computer monitor or profit-and-loss sheet.

11. Spend at least 10 percent of your workday making eye contact with customers and employees.

12. Finally, say please and thank you. Require your team to say please and thank you to each other and customers. Don't forget to say you're welcome, too.

I could write a book dedicated to the kindness mindset, but you get the point. For now, take the time to jot down a few of these kindness shifts in your notes and start practicing uncommon kindness in your leadership.

When you show kindness, you foster a sense of confidence in your employees, who believe they can accomplish more. And they do. As the kindness mindset settles in, it leads to your team embracing the next mindset: the courageous mindset.

Courageous Mindset

Kindness is relatively easy to understand and define, but how would you define a courageous mindset? For our purposes, courage is a willingness to accept and adapt to changes. In facing difficulties and change, courage brings long-term success and hope for yourself and those you lead.

When you are courageous as a leader, those you lead are far more willing to follow. Many have heard or read the classic story of David and Goliath from the Bible. Here we see the heart of David and his courage:

> David said to Saul, "Let no one lose heart on account of this Philistine; your servant will go and fight him."
>
> Saul replied, "You are not able to go out against this Philistine and fight him; you are only a young man, and he has been a warrior from his youth."
>
> But David said to Saul, "Your servant has been keeping his father's sheep. When a lion or a bear came and carried off a sheep from the flock, I went after it, struck it, and rescued the sheep from its mouth. When it turned on me, I seized it by its hair, struck it, and killed it. Your servant has killed both the lion and the bear; this uncircumcised Philistine will be like one of them because he has defied the armies of the living God. The Lord who rescued me from the paw of the lion and the paw of the bear will rescue me from the hand of this Philistine." (1 Samuel 17:32–37 NIV)

There are many books written on the topics of courage and courageous leadership. Five things stand out in this story about David. First, David did this for the people, so that "no one [would] lose heart on account of this Philistine."

Second, David led by being courageous. How are you being bold for your employees and the customers you serve? His previous acts of courage—going up against lions and bears—allowed him to stand up in this moment and be courageous. The practice built confidence, and the confidence built his courage.

Third, he knew what he could do, which gave him the confidence and faith to step into this unknown situation. David knew he had the weaponry and skills to win. Later in this story, David swings his sling around his head, and it picks up enough speed to sink a rock into Goliath's head and kill him.

Fourth, David had been training for this moment (even if he didn't know it) for years. What skills do you need to develop? What skills are you developing that will give you courage when you need it?

Finally, and most importantly, David had faith in something bigger than himself, and he was humble enough to believe that God would give him success for Israel just as He'd given David success in protecting his sheep.

There were five things that prepared David for this moment.

- ☑ He was all about his people (not himself).
- ☑ He was courageous because he loved his people.
- ☑ He was aware of his skills.
- ☑ He'd been training for this moment (even if he didn't know it).
- ☑ He believed in something bigger than himself.

What gives you faith to step out in the scary moments for your people, customers, and business?

■ Courage as a Skill

Courage is not always displayed in a heroic act of rescue or defying the odds as David did. Sometimes courage is less noticeable. Courage is a skill you can learn, and it enables you to make high-risk decisions. You hone the skill of courage over time. It's a combination of experience, intuition, and timing.

You can develop courage by applying the following six steps and responding to the questions that accompany each step.

1. *Set goals.* What are you trying to achieve here? David set the goal of killing the giant to prove to the Philistines that the God of Israel was more powerful than Goliath.

2. *Determine the impact of your goals.* What is the effect of not pursuing this? If David had not stepped up, the Israelites probably would've eventually acceded to the Philistines and become their slaves.

3. *Take a stand and have the right people on your side.* In David's case, God was on his side. Who can help you achieve this courageous act (goal)?

4. *Look at the risks and benefits.* Who will win? Who will lose? Can it be a win-win? David knew his win would be a win for his nation, making the risk worth it.

5. *Get the timing right.* When should I pick this fight? When should I take this risk? David was simply bringing his brothers some sandwiches when he saw Goliath for the first time. He weighed his options, evaluated the impact and goals, reflected on his skill, and went for it.

6. *Finally, have a contingency plan in place.* What happens if this fails? What happens if this works out? David didn't plan to fail, but he knew that other consequences could follow. David picked up five smooth stones. Many believe this wasn't a contingency in the event he missed, but for Goliath's four brothers! But the fact he was prepared for more than one shot tells he was prepared for a different outcome.

Courage is a powerful mindset you can develop. When you put all six of these steps in place, courage is sure to follow. Combining these steps with knowing your vision and values, and then having the integrity to act on them, is key to leadership and foundational to the self-awareness and growth pillars.

Next, we look at the importance of the collaborative mindset.

Collaborative Mindset

On April 11, 1970, *Apollo 13* launched for the third moon-landing mission. The goal was to place three astronauts on the lunar surface. Fifty-six hours into the flight, an oxygen tank explosion forced the crew to abandon all thoughts of reaching the moon and focus on getting back to earth alive.

James Lovell, Fred Haise, and John "Jack" Swigert were the three astronauts.

"Houston, we've had a problem."

The design of the Apollo spacecraft—the orbiter *Odyssey* and the lander *Aquarius*—was comprised of two spacecraft joined by a tunnel. On their flight to the moon, the crew lived in the *Odyssey*.

On April 13, when the crew was about 200,000 miles from Earth and approaching the moon, an employee at NASA's Mission Control Center spotted a low-pressure warning signal on a hydrogen tank.

The signal might have indicated a failure or simply suggested that the hydrogen was getting close to freezing. The solution was a reasonably straightforward fix called a "cryo stir." This procedure would heat and fan the gas within the tank to keep the gas from freezing.

Jack Swigert started the procedure and then suddenly the entire spacecraft shook. The cryo stir had failed. The oxygen pressure dropped, and the spacecraft was now without power. Alarm lights illuminated in *Odyssey* and at Mission Control. With a tone of concern, Swigert simply said, "Houston, we've had a problem."

In a post-analysis, NASA determined that wires in the oxygen tank created a spark and caused a fire just before takeoff. The fire pulled one oxygen tank from its place and damaged another within the spacecraft, and the preflight inspections had missed these exposed wires.

The spacecraft's control thrusters had detected the leaking oxygen and attempted to keep it steady by firing little bursts. When several jets were slammed shut by the blast, the thruster system failed. As a result, there was a significant reduction in *Odyssey's* power and ability to maneuver.

Fortunately, the astronauts could access the *Aquarius* module. It was the capsule intended to land on the moon, not to reenter the earth's atmosphere. Because *Aquarius* didn't have a heat shield, Lovell and Haise had to bring the lunar module up and operational before Swigert could go back into *Odyssey* to conserve power for splashdown on Earth.

■ The Cold, Miserable Trip Home

The crew had to overcome two significant obstacles to get home and maintain power in *Aquarius*. The astronauts had to switch off every nonessential system in the spacecraft after completing the critical burn to direct the spacecraft back towards Earth.

Without heat, in this case a nonessential system, the cabin rapidly fell to near-freezing temperatures. In addition, the near-freezing temperatures damaged their food supply. To make matters worse, the crew had to limit water consumption to ensure that *Aquarius*, which was operating beyond its intended duration, would have enough liquid to cool its hardware. And if things were not bad enough, *Aquarius* was only intended to carry two people, not three.

Back on Earth, NASA flight director Gene Kranz pulled his shift of controllers off regular rotation to help the crew strategize how they could maximize water, power, and breathable air.

While the world watched, I team faced an impossibly difficult task with so many variables and people involved and lives at stake. Over the course of the next four days the astronauts endured tremendous physical hardships. All three astronauts lost weight, and Haise developed a kidney infection. What looked impossible turned out to be possible as *Aquarius* entered Earth's atmosphere without burning up. On April 17, Lovell, Haise, and Swigert splashed down successfully in the Pacific Ocean near Samoa.

This remarkable story illustrates the power of teamwork and collaboration. The actions and quick thinking of everyone involved saved the lives of these three astronauts. This story illustrates so many lessons about the power of collaboration. Let's look at five.

1. Communication
The back-and-forth communication between the *Apollo 13* crew and Houston was vital in the crew's survival. The ground crew only had radio communication to walk the astronauts through rewiring a spacecraft for survival. Clear communication must happen before, during, and after any task if success is the objective.

2. Learning from Mistakes
Quick thinking and innovative solutions rescued the crew, along with lessons learned from previous Apollo successes and failures. Everyone's experience was valued equally, and the combination of their collective experience is what allowed them to be successful.

After this event, NASA made numerous design modifications to the service module and command module. These modifications undoubtedly aided future missions.

3. Teamwork
The teamwork of the astronauts, NASA, and the engineering and design crew saved lives. The round-the-clock efforts of these teams allowed this story to be NASA's "finest hour" instead of a tragic ending.

4. Quality

Ultimately, manufacturing and testing mistakes created a malfunction, and the spark from an exposed wire had caused the fire. Despite this mistake, the collective efforts made it possible to salvage the situation. The crew returned safely to Earth, proving the quality of the remaining systems, processes, and materials. In an ideal collaboration, quality will be maintained or increased.

5. Innovation

Innovation was vital to Apollo 13. In-flight innovations saved lives and would ultimately improve future missions as well. Your team likely has hundreds of simple innovations that could positively shift your business. Significant innovations will also occur if you make the time and collaborate consistently.

This story illustrates the power of collaboration in a high-stakes situation, but I realize it's not always roses and butterflies in business.

■ The Fighting Brothers

A man had three hard-working sons that frequently got into fights. Their fighting had gotten so bad that their neighbors made jokes about them. Even though the father tried to help his children make peace, he could never succeed.

Frustrated, the father implored his sons to learn how to collaborate, but they refused. The father then resolved to solve the problem and hopefully impart a practical lesson for his sons to forget their differences and become a cohesive unit.

"I'll give you each an equal bundle of sticks to break in two," the father informed his sons. "The one who breaks the wood fastest will be rewarded." This task took the sons mere minutes to complete, but they started to fight about who'd finished first.

"Boys, the work isn't done yet," the father added. "Each of you will receive ten more sticks, but you must break them in half while in a bundle rather than breaking each one separately."

The sons tried their best, but they could not break the bundles in half. They returned to their father and told him that it was an impossible task.

The father said, "Now you've seen how hard it is to break all ten of them when they're bundled together. If the three of you stay together and work as a team, no one will be able to break you. If you fight all the time and stand divided, anybody will be able to break you."

■ Collaboration How-To

To create a collaboration mindset in your organization, set expectations. Get everyone on the same page. Create communication channels through chat apps, project management tools, and emails to ensure everyone understands expectations. Create clearly defined job scorecards for each person. Define how to use each tool and the systems in your organization.

You can also use productivity tools that allow your team to share tasks and ideas. Slack is a great example. Having a central project management tool is vital to communicating across teams and maintaining expectations/standards. My preference is Todoist.

Whatever tools you use, the key is to define how your business operates and track your long-term goals. A combination of communication tools provides three things.

- Task management software like Todoist provides employees with reference tools for procedures and systems.
- Apps like Slack, Loom, and Teams enable real-time communication.
- Programs like Google Sheets, Excel, and Project Management apps allow your team to track and share results in real time.

When you put all these pieces together, you unlock productivity and reduce stress, which in turn benefits your team and customers.

But beware: It is easy to create a business context of death by meetings. When you follow the Perfect Meeting approach, meetings become enjoyable and highly productive.

■ The Perfect Meeting Agenda

Following are a few tips to create a Perfect Meeting.:

1. Stick with the meeting agenda. If "emergencies" come up, they need to be addressed in a later meeting.
2. As much as possible, schedule meetings as reoccurring events for a specific day and time.
3. Each team member should provide a progress report on actions assigned from the previous meeting.

4. When an agenda item requires discussion, every member is given an uninterrupted time to share their thoughts/perspectives (2-3 minutes).

5. If clear action items aren't apparent, repeat the uninterrupted around the room discussion.

6. From the discussion, clear action items for meeting members will then be defined and documented.

7. Confirm the next meeting date/time for follow up and progress reports on on agenda itmes.

As the meeting leader, you are responsible to hold the meeting context to give everyone time and space to think. Each person is afforded the opportunity to share and be heard. It sounds like a drawn out process, but in reality, it makes meetings more efficient and produces higher quality actions. Other ways to support a Perfect Meeting.

- Support them by asking open-ended questions (more on this later in the chapter).
- Use the WISER listener approach.
- Create an environment where people genuinely share their thoughts on a topic.
- Create space for people to have time to think and be heard.
- Each meeting should end with people knowing their next actions and expectations.

With Perfect Meetings and reasonably sized teams, a meetings can shirk in duration and in some cases, may only take twenty to thirty minutes instead of 60-90 minutes. The beauty of these meetings is that they are supportive, collaborative, and action-oriented.

As you reflect on what it means to have a collaborative mindset, make a few notes on where you excel. I also encourage you to start today to roll out the Perfect Meeting Agenda in your business to see what results you get.

Just as the courageous mindset often follows the kindness mindset, the beauty of the collaborative mindset is the innovation that often follows. The Perfect Meeting plan will help set the context for innovation.

Innovative Mindset

In 1975, Kodak invented the first digital camera. This camera was way ahead of its time and a remarkable feat of technology. But we all know who became the leader in digital camera technology: Apple.

So, what happened to all the advances Kodak had made? Well, because was filmless photography, and Kodak management's reaction was, "That's cute—but don't tell anyone about it. Remember, we're in the film-making business, not the camera business." They didn't see it as innovation, but something that required too much work and wasn't a fit for the market.

Interestingly, the story of missing the innovation opportunity doesn't end there. In 1981, the CEO of Kodak began an extensive study into the viability of digital cameras. They found there would need to be a ten-year ramp up for the market and manufacturing of digital cameras to become standard.

You would think the timeline would be great news. After all, Kodak was ahead of the curve. They were already at the forefront of technology and had the capital to invest. All their research indicated it was the path photography was on, and they had ten years to prepare.

The problem was they didn't innovate. Kodak didn't implement the necessary changes, and as a result, filed for bankruptcy in 2012, thirty-one years after their own research had revealed digital photography as a great opportunity.

The story of Kodak shows the tragedy of not innovating. They stumbled through decades of changes and shifts in the marketplace, but with the management unwilling to innovate, they lost out on a multi-billion-dollar industry.

You may not run a multi-billion-dollar company, but in your own way, on your own scale, you could make the same innovation mistakes. What could you do today to create a culture of innovation in your business? Below is a list of five ways to develop an innovation mindset across your team.

■ Every Idea Is Valued

Create a culture where every idea is valued. If an employee is brave enough to bring you an innovative idea, there's likely to be at least some nugget of value you can apply. Recognizing the one idea they brought you is likely to encourage them to share many more. In fact, there are likely dozens of simple and innovative ideas that your team has in mind, but they'll never see the light of day if you don't draw them out and then practice the habit of listening!

When you invite people to share their ideas and create a sense of safety around sharing ideas, no matter how wild it might sound on the surface, you build a culture of innovation. Also, the ideas don't have to disrupt multi-billion or multi-million-dollar industries. The idea could be as simple as the way you serve, manufacture, or sell.

Most ideas won't be earth-shattering, but having a mindset of innovation sets the stage for dozens of small ideas to create significant improvements. Having a mindset of innovation starts with having an open mind to new ideas. No matter how the message is delivered or who delivers it, the cumulative effect of saying yes to new ideas and exploring them leads to innovation.

■ The Lazy Employee

Understand the difference between a lazy employee and an innovative employee. When I was working at the Thousand Hills Pet Resort, an employee surprised me with some interesting comments. She said, "Kyle, I probably shouldn't be telling my boss this, but I'm lazy. But lazy people are efficient. I hate doing things over and over." Then she shared an idea for creating a much smoother flow in feeding the dogs.

We implemented that employee's process that day. As far as I know, the pet resort still uses this feeding process. This employee wasn't lazy. She was creative and innovative. She believed in working smarter, not just harder. Fortunately, I could see she was innovative and not lazy and was willing to try her idea without judgment.

■ Failure Is Okay

Innovation will NOT happen if your team does not feel safe to fail or share their "lazy" ideas with you. Team members need to know that you not only trust them, but trust them enough to try their ideas, even if implementing them results in failure. Building trust means you need to set the example by being willing to try out-of-the-box ideas, and then reassuring them that you're ok if those ideas fail.

As a small business owner, you set the tone for future innovations when you show you trust your employees. As I shared with you in the pet resort story, innovation is worth it. That feeding innovation made it possible to have one employee prepare food instead of two, which created a more efficient workflow, freed up more people to take care of pets and customers, and resulted in saving thousands of dollars.

■ Questions and Angles

I mentioned previously to "think like a beginner" and "to think big and bigger." When you also look at everything from multiple angles, this approach will help solidify an innovation mindset in yourself and your employees.

You shift your perspective by creating an open, question-asking culture. Allow people to be comfortable asking about what you do, how you do it, and why. For example, if you've always followed the same procedures with customers, what- and why-based questions can help you discover opportunities for innovation.

■ Take Action Quickly

Most of the time, innovations are small and will have few consequences if they fail. But if they succeed, these small innovations an bring about significant changes over time.

Every small business owner wants to be more effective and efficient with their time. The beauty of minor innovations is that they nearly always save businesses time. If small changes can create more efficiency and save time, why not implement them quickly?

If implementing the idea requires significant changes, it may take more time, but even small trials of the idea are worth exploring for the potential big payoff. Once there's a clear pattern of results from investigating the idea, you can begin full implementation of all the changes that are required.

■ Look At Patterns

Sometimes, innovation can be found by considering past mistakes you have made in your business. Looking at past processes that didn't work, people that didn't fit your culture, or failed marketing approaches, you might find patterns in these mistakes. Those patterns can provide clues for innovation.

Take a moment to look at your business and consider what has been wildly successful in the past. Now also look for patterns in these successes.

- ➲ Who have you worked best with?
- ➲ What services pleased your customers?
- ➲ What communication has worked well?
- ➲ Which employees performed the best?

As you recognize these patterns, make sure to ask open-ended questions about what did and didn't work, and then act. Don't be like Kodak! When Kodak asked these questions and found answers that pointed toward acting and didn't, it was the start of their future failure.

The innovative mindset reveals the power of asking questions. The inability of leaders to ask the right questions of themselves and their employees is the number one cause of stress, low efficiency, and burnout.

How do you know what questions to ask? You must leverage a coaching mindset in your leadership. I have placed the coaching mindset last in this chapter because it gives your leadership house its shine. Developing a coaching mindset in your leadership keeps your Leadership House windows clean and your doors open.

If you don't coach your employees, you cannot become an empowering leader. Let's look at how you can use this final mindset to unlock the potential of all your influence in your leadership house.

Coaching Mindset

In Timothy Gallwey's book The Inner Game of Tennis, he shares a story about the power of coaching. A local resort had overbooked the tennis class at one of their courts and needed more instructors.

So, the resort brought in a couple of ski instructors. What happened when the ski instructors coached the tennis students might surprise you.

Most people would assume calamity and failure would be the natural results. The opposite happened. The ski instructors who coached the tennis players did just as well, and in some cases, got better results than the tennis coaches!

The tennis coaches had technical knowledge and experience, so they spent much of their time critiquing and instructing the students and rarely asking questions. But the inexperienced ski instructors, who lacked technical knowledge, only had one option: They had to rely on the players' self-diagnosis. They could not be the expert or answer any of their questions. They had to get feedback from the students by asking questions.

The tennis coaches were only tackling the problems they noticed in each tennis player's game. The ski instructors who became tennis coaches were coaching, not problem-solving. The difference was the tennis instructors coached the problem, and the ski instructors coached the person.

In other words, when the students were coached by being asked open-ended questions, it helped them to reflect on what they were doing and the results they wanted. This helped them determine how to solve the problem in their technique, and the new awareness stuck because it came from within. Overall, this coaching approach proved more successful than when players were critiqued and told what to do.

When I tried to coach my daughter in soccer with almost zero personal soccer experience, I was clearly not the best choice to coach a young soccer player just starting out.

After my nine-year-old's first soccer season, it was evident that telling her what to do did not improve her game. However, helping her discover how to get better by asking open-ended questions created leaps in her ability. By the end of the season, she was scoring goals and had become a key player on the team.

■ What Is Coaching?

The tennis student example above illustrates the power of coaching. But before we go any further, I feel a clear definition of coaching is in order. But first, the approach I advocate is not the Bill Belichick, Nick Saban, or even John Wooden kind of coaching.

Coaching is an intentional conversation entered into for the discovery of new insights and awareness through the power of questions and deep listening.

Let me point out what's not in this definition: telling an employee what to do, offering options for people to choose from, dictating ideas and perspectives, sharing advice, or giving an opinion.

I'm not an idiot. I realize that a business owner needs to provide answers, offer opinions, and give options. But there are beautiful moments of opportunity every day to coach your team members. When these moments present themselves, they call for you to have an intentional conversation. Within that conversation, you will empower your employees and unlock the awareness, mindsets, and hidden talents that your employees need to use not only for the current problem but for potential future problems they may encounter.

Here are a few examples of when/where these intentional conversations can occur:

- ⮑ When someone knocks on your office door
- ⮑ During a one-to-one or group meeting
- ⮑ On-site, when someone asks you a question you know the answer to
- ⮑ During a casual lunch conversation
- ⮑ While you are brainstorming a product or service
- ⮑ When completing an employee review
- ⮑ When training new employees
- ⮑ During an accountability conversation

These intentional coaching conversations can last from two to twenty minutes. In the workplace, they are generally informal and unexpected. But within those two to twenty minutes spent coaching can be gold for your business.

It is in these moments that you truly listen to your team members and invest in them. They will share insights and offer perspectives that could prove invaluable to help your business move forward. You can't manufacture the trust, respect, and loyalty created in these conversations. You must be intentional and committed to the coaching process.

Coaching team members also saves you from carrying the burden of being the one with all the answers. Coaching can keep you from hours of inefficient work because your team has a problem-solving perspective on your business that you alone don't have.

Developing a coaching leadership style saves you from the painful process of replacing people who leave the team out of frustration with a leader who doesn't listen. Coaching can also keep you from many mistakes and unforeseen circumstances because team members become proactive. When you invest in growing and coaching, you build better team members and speed up new-hire training because team members are shown how to find solutions on their own. This list of the benefits of coaching could go on almost indefinitely.

The point is when you have these intentional coaching conversations, it will do wonders for you, your team members, and your business's bottom line. Here's how and why.

■ The Power of Questions

Most leaders operate from the perspective of being experts and a source of knowledge, not from a perspective of curiosity and being a lifelong learner. I've heard this perspective called "know-it-all-ism." When leaders interact with employees, board members, and colleagues, a 60/40 ratio will serve them amazingly well—that is, they listen 60 percent of the time and speak the other 40 percent. In coaching, this ratio shifts to 80/20.

Here's why:

- ➲ Answers are built on the past, while questions focus on and bring about the future.
- ➲ Answers are rigid, while questions create flexibility.
- ➲ Answers limit people and situations, whereas questions open possibilities.
- ➲ Answers make people stick with what works. Questions create innovation.
- ➲ Answers create experts and superiority. Questions require humility and a learner mindset.

When you look at your knowledge and experience based on this, questions become a much more valuable use of your time in conversations. This does not mean to play dumb. But instead, leverage your knowledge and turn what you know into powerful, open-ended questions. To help you learn this approach, I've created what I call ABC Street of coaching.

■ Five Keys to the Coaching Mindset: ABC ST.

1. **A**sk open-ended questions.
2. **B**e okay with long silences.
3. **C**uriosity creates new awareness.
4. **S**hut Up so you can...
5. **T**ruly listen.

Ask open-ended questions. A coaching mindset requires you to ask questions that are not leading people to the answer you want or closed questions that lead to answers like "yes or no." During these powerful coaching conversations, the questions you ask should be open-ended and will lead to insights or new awareness.

Open-ended questions are powerful. They make people think and help them arrive at new perspectives. Open-ended questions help people go on a journey of discovery. These journeys unlock new learning and attitudes. They also will provide you with unique insights and business opportunities.

Closed vs. Open Questions

- Closed: "Have you considered talking to the customer?"
  - Open: "Who could you talk to about this?"

- Closed: "Have you considered doing X?
  - Open: "What are your options?"

- Closed: "Did you follow the procedure?"
  - Open: "How can you learn to do this?"

- Closed: "Did you look online?"
  - Open: "What are some possible resources?"

Open-ended questions typically start with how, what and who. The how questions generally lead to action, and the what and who questions lead to discovery. Also, when asking questions, keep them short. Few words make for fewer leading questions

Be present. Be okay with silences. Here are two rules that will help you keep quiet and allow for self-discovery.

Remember the WAIT acronym? Use the eight-second rule and apply the "Why Am I Talking?" question. If you find yourself responding and talking when the situation could become an intentional coaching conversation, remember the first rule to shut up and then use the W.A.I.T. technique.

As a reminder, the eight-second rule means after you ask an open-ended question and before you say anything, give the other person eight seconds to respond. The eight-seconds rule comes from studies AT&T did on what people do when the phone goes silent.

If a phone goes silent for four seconds, the person will ask, "Are you still there?" If the line goes quiet for eight seconds, they will hang up. The reality is people need time to think. If you ask multiple questions or don't leave room for silence, the insight or new awareness will not have time to come to the surface. So, ask and then wait for at least eight seconds.

Curiosity. A BLUE Shirt Leader with a coaching mindset starts with curiosity and a genuine desire to listen to people's responses. Curiosity is the key to opening new awareness. If you ask a question and expect a specific reply, you aren't listening for their insight. You are simply asking a rhetorical question.

Curiosity allows you to explore further and dive in with more questions to pull out your employees' insights and ideas. Curiosity often looks like believing each of your employees has something to contribute to the team beyond the basics of the work they do.

Shut your mouth: Shutting up also means shutting down your assumptions about this conversation and person. It also means shutting down your ego and expertise. You can better coach in these moments when you limit your internal and external chatter.

Shutting your mouth and being quiet does not equal listening. Similarly, silence does not equal listening, but it is the preparation point that allows you to listen. Listening is an active process.

Truly listen: Truly listening is a whole-body experience for you and them. At the beginning of the book, I described four different communication channels. While engaging in these brief conversations, tune into all four channels. Pay attention to the words they speak, the tone of their words, and their body language. Additionally, make sure to tune into the fourth channel of intuition (your gut).

Listening requires your undivided attention to the individual and a willingness to stay in the moment. When you listen, listen to understand, and then look for meaning and new awareness, not for yourself but for the person you are listening to.

■ Conclusion

The coaching mindset will create a desire to help others experience new perspectives and insights. All good conversations are ultimately about awareness, not necessarily action.

When a coaching opportunity comes up, your job is to help the other person gain a new understanding and awareness. It is not about pushing your agenda or perspective.

The coaching mindset is one of the most powerful tools in this entire book. Take the time to look again at the list of potential coaching scenarios. Picture these happening in your workplace and picture yourself applying the mindsets from this chapter.

Empowerment is the part of your Leadership House that attracts others to you. It's the windows and doors to your leadership house that allow others to look in.

- ➲ The kindness mindset creates the warmth and welcoming spirit of your leadership house.

- ➲ A courageous mindset helps your team and business be flexible and adaptable in times of change. Courage gives people the opening to collaborate with you to know you will listen to them and welcome their ideas.

- ➲ A collaborative mindset sparks new ideas and synergies that speed up productivity and effectiveness.

- ➲ An innovative mindset opens the door to not just new ideas but business-changing and revenue-altering ideas. To get to this place, you need a combination of kindness, courage, and collaboration.

- ➲ Finally, we come to the coaching mindset. Leadership is fundamentally about leading people, not things. Metaphorically, the coaching mindset serves as the thermostat of your leadership house. The coaching mindset will empower you to control the temperature better than any other mindset.

In the next chapter we will look at five habits to help you become an empowering leader. These habits are some of the most challenging practices to adopt, but as with the mindsets shared in this chapter, they will help you and your business tremendously.

Chapter 10:

You Have the Power to Empower

BLUE Shirt know and show the way, but they don't stay in the way.

Leadership is a challenging dance. It's a dance of knowing your skill level and patterns and your partner's.

A few years into our marriage, my wife and I decided it would be fun to take swing dance lessons. It seemed like it would be easy enough. After several weeks of classes and practicing at home, we went to a couple of swing dance events. That was when things got interesting.

When we hit the dance floor, there was so much to remember. We had to start on the proper count and keep our feet from tripping over one another as we tried different moves. We tried to look like we knew what we were doing. But we struggled to have any natural rhythm or style. It was fun, and we enjoyed the time together, but we were far from winning any dance competitions.

Since then, we've danced a few times together, and it's always fun to dance with my wife. But the dancing lasts sixty seconds or so before we start giggling (mostly her) and can't find the beat again.

Many entrepreneurs are like my wife and me when it comes to leadership. They've had some sort of exposure to leadership training and development and put some of it into practice but then stumble with implementation. Once they fall out of rhythm, they walk off the dance floor and go back to what they know, which ends up not working very well.

If we are going to empower a team of people to run our business and do it successfully, we need to get a lot of time on the dance floor, so to speak. When you watch great dancers, there's a certain rhythm and flow to their dance. It seems almost effortless. They glide to the rhythm of the music and anticipate what is coming. BLUE Shirt Leaders do this as well.

My wife and I didn't look too great because of our lack of practice and the imperfect implementation of what we learned in our dance classes. In leadership, your dance partners are your employees. If you don't practice the mindsets and habits mentioned in this book, your dance partners and you will look silly, and the rhythm and flow won't be there.

Not only do you need to practice and study the mindsets and habits mentioned in this book, but you can help your dance partners do the same.

■ Dancing Into Empowerment

In this chapter, I want to help you create a rhythm and flow to leading to make it easy for your team to follow. The first empowerment habit is to know your dance partner. What makes them smile? What is uncomfortable for them? What can you do to help them shine?

The second empowerment habit is about communication. On the dance floor, the communication in dance is nuanced between partners. There's a subtle nudge, a tug, a pull, or a look that keeps the partners in sync. Make sure your team isn't afraid to tug or pull and lead the way with an idea. Give your team clear permission to communicate about where they see themselves and the business, and to give you feedback to help you better connect as partners.

The third empowerment habit is practice time. Your team needs resources. They need the opportunities to practice and the tools to perform well. In other words, your dance partners need the right environment, energy, and equipment to achieve what you want them to execute smoothly.

The fourth empowerment habit is giving them the stage, also known as delegation. You can't always be there with a dance partner. Sometimes they will go off and practice or even perform with someone else. When you practice delegation, you move to being the coach and not the partner, stepping out of the way to let your team shine.

Finally, when you stick to the BLUE Shirt Leadership Framework, success will follow. Celebrate these successes. However, if you and your team aren't toe-stomping or banging knees from time to time, you aren't taking enough risk. Without risk, you'll never experience the robust growth that follows. Make sure to celebrate when things go well and keep going when you stumble. As the leader, you must own the mistakes and share the victories.

The first empowerment habit requires that you know the people on your team exceptionally well. You need to study them to understand their skills, as well as the patterns and quirks of how they perform.

The Study Habit

By using assessments and an observant mindset, you can understand someone's unique communication style. The more you study and understand how each person expresses themselves and receives information, the easier it will be for you to lead them.

DISC is a behavior assessment tool that has helped me understand and serve my clients for several years. It's what I call the "cheat code" to understand people.

Within the DISC framework, there are four core styles. Most people have two of these styles that are predominant in their personalities. I share with many of my clients that we all may speak the same language, but everyone's style differs. DISC helps you understand the dialect of everyone on your team so that you can better communicate with one another.

Knowing the DISC framework is a huge key in helping you implement empowerment habits. Here's a summary of the four styles to help you think about people on your team and your own style. Let's look at them with the analogy of gears in a car.

■ Dominance/D Style

The Dominance Style (D Style) is like being in drive.

Strengths: People with a high D score are driven, they are in the gear of drive. They look straight ahead out the windshield. They rarely look back. They are problem solvers and want to get from A to B as fast as possible with a return on their efforts.

Limitations: D Style people are not great with touchy-feely stuff. They can get a little too competitive at times. They are very assertive and direct. Sometimes this style can be over-controlling. They fear losing control.

Who in your leadership house shows Dominance Style behaviors?

■ Influence/I Style

The Influence Style (I Style) is in four-wheel drive.

Strengths: People with a high I score are adventurous and energetic. They can overcome challenges and obstacles. When you are interacting with an I Style, it's about fun and excitement. This style loves to have fun and get attention. Their primary need is to interact. It's not as fun to go off-roading by yourself! This style is highly talkative and social.

Limitations: I Style people struggle with details and follow-through. Too often, they share an opinion without being asked. They will also struggle with needing approval, avoiding conflicts, and may not do well with a lot of structure. They have fears of failure, not being liked, and being mis-characterized.

Who in your leadership house shows Influence Style behaviors?

■ Steady/S Style

The Steady Style (S Style) prefers the gear of neutral.

Strengths: People with a high S score prefer to coast in neutral. They don't want to drive. They want to keep conflict down, prefer control over chaos, and like things to stay the same. They are the stabilizers and the peacemakers of a group. They are responders to situations. This gear means they are pushed and pulled more than the other styles. The S Style is also the most patient.

S Style people are cooperative and supportive. Sometimes they need a bit of a nudge to pick up the pace. Their primary need is safety and stability.

Limitations: S Style people struggle with being flexible or changing. Sometimes they are indecisive or overly submissive. They have a difficult time standing up for their wants and needs in a group. They may be difficult to "read." They may be in neutral, but the brakes still work.

Who in your leadership house shows Steady Style behaviors?

■ Conscientious/C Style

Conscientious Style (C Style) people are in the gear of Reverse.

Strengths: People with a high C score take in all the details and information. When you put a car in reverse you need to use all mirrors, the windshield, backup cameras, and anything else available to gain the information you need to move safely. C Style people like to analyze and review. They follow procedures, protocols, and policies. They look for logic and standards and data is their comfort zone.

Limitations: C Styles struggle with people that are impulsive in their decision-making. They can be a bit critical of others. They tend to get analysis paralysis. They fear being wrong or not having the "right" answer.

Who under your leadership house shows Conscientious Style behaviors?

All people are a blend of styles but in varying intensities. They each have a main style. Admittedly, you can't comprehensively know a person's personality and behaviors because of an assessment. However, you will gain new insights by understanding their style. Using the DISC framework to gain insights will help you to adjust your style to fit others a bit better, and just like in dancing, style counts!

Before I share a story of the power of the DISC framework, let me encourage you to review the coaching mindset section in the previous chapter. Those tips will help you study your team and understand them better. At BLUE Shirt Coaching, we can provide DISC assessments for your team.

■ The Accountable Leader Habit

As a coach, I sometimes share harsh truths with clients. When you can talk about someone's leadership objectively using an assessment tool like DISC, you can cut through a lot of bs and quickly get to the heart of things.

For example, I once met with the twelve-person office team of a multi-million-dollar construction firm where I was going over DISC styles. The meeting had been going on for about seventy-five minutes when it came time for me to speak some harsh truths. We were in a room with a large, eighty-inch TV mounted on the wall on one end and two wood-framed glass doors on the other. Seated at the giant oak table sat the twelve team members discussing being behind on projects and not being nearly as efficient as they could be.

We were making some progress in discovering the cause and determining a better path forward when we realized that the habits of the CEO were the tipping point of what needed to change. He knew this. We all knew this. There hadn't been much change occurring over the last few months, and the cause was clear.

I'd been studying this leader and his team for a while, and I knew the weight of what I was about to say. But I needed the CEO to get uncomfortable in front of his team if anything was going to change.

I looked at the CEO and said, "Tom, if you want your team to be more accountable for their responsibilities, you need to be more accountable for yours." After an awkward pause and a few moments of reflection, Tom said, "You're right. I need to be more accountable, so the team will too."

Since that meeting, a couple of employees have left. They hired some A+ talent and are locking in new systems to improve accountability and efficiency. As a bonus, their revenue numbers are the highest they've ever been.

If you take time to study your team, you will know when to say and do what you need to do. You will be able to read the room and make the right move. But this only works because you've been studying your dance partners for weeks, months, or even years and you know when to give the nudge, tug, or outright directive.

It may not be comfortable, but that one moment of making the CEO uncomfortable made all the difference. It was just one move, and now the dance can go on smoother and more focused than before.

The overwhelmingly common habit of BLUE Shirt Leaders is the next habit. It's an obvious one, but not everyone leverages this habit as they should.

The Over-Communication Habit

The findings are striking. 42 percent of employees don't understand or even know their company's vision, mission, or values when it comes to communication. Twenty-five percent of employees say they can't trust their employer. Fifty percent of employees feel like they're not getting all the information and facts needed to succeed in their roles .

Ninety-one percent of managers in the U.S. say a candidate's alignment with the company culture is equal to or more important than skills and experience. Employees are 26 percent more likely to leave their jobs if they feel a lack of respect from colleagues. Okay, enough stats .

The important part is that these statistics show that employees, leaders, and candidates need to communicate more. The shift occurs in recognizing and acting on the need to over communicate everything and anything that you want to see your team and business achieve.

Without a doubt, when you follow the mindsets and habits explained in this book and consistently implement them, the habit of over communication will be second nature. You will know what to communicate and how often.

Remember our discussion on goal setting and then creating a purposeful cadence of accountability around this goal? That accountability tactic is what leaders need to utilize to communicate with and empower their team members.

■ We Choose to Go to the Moon

On a hot summer day at Rice University on September 12, 1962, President John F. Kennedy spoke to a group gathered there. This was during an unprecedented time in our history as a country. The United States was locked in a cold war and a space race with the Soviet Union, and there was much at stake.

With the potential for missiles to be launched from outer space and strike our country, we needed a unifying message and a way to make the war so costly for the Soviets that they could not continue. The space race was a matter of national pride and protection.

President Kennedy's speech was summed up in one line and a clear vision: "We choose to go to the moon."

Here is part of his speech beginning about seven minutes in:

> We set sail on this new sea because there is new knowledge to be gained, and new rights to be won, and they must be won and used for the progress of all people. Space science, like nuclear science and all technology, has no conscience of its own. Whether it will become a force for good or ill depends on man, and only if the United States occupies a position of pre-eminence can we help decide whether this new ocean will be a sea of peace or a new terrifying theater of war. I do not say that we should or will go unprotected against the hostile misuse of space any more than we go unprotected against the hostile use of land or sea, but I do say that space can be explored and mastered without feeding the fires of war, without repeating the mistakes that man has made in extending his writ around this globe of ours.

> There is no strife, no prejudice, no national conflict in outer space as yet. Its hazards are hostile to us all. Its conquest deserves the best of all mankind, and its opportunity for peaceful cooperation may never come again. But why, some say, the Moon? Why choose this as our goal? And they may well ask, why climb the highest mountain? Why, thirty-five years ago, fly the Atlantic? Why does Rice play Texas?

> We choose to go to the moon. We choose to go to the moon. ... We choose to go to the moon in this decade and do the other things, not because they are easy, but because they are hard; because that goal will serve to organize and measure the best of our energies and skills, because that challenge is one that we are willing to accept, one we are unwilling to postpone, and one we intend to win, and the others, _too_ .

This speech unified a team of scientists, chemists, manufacturers, engineers, and more to ultimately achieve this vision when on July 20, 1969, man first landed on the moon. Some people argue about why the United States went to the moon and the ultimate benefit, but this central message remained a focal point that eventually got us to the moon.

Is it true that the vision had to overcome concerns, resistance from the public, and objections to the $40 billion price tag? Yes. However, while these reservations persisted, so did the message. In fact, the message remained even after John F. Kennedy's assassination.

The message won. We landed on the moon. The USA became the clear leader in the space race and the technology used to reach the moon is still relevant today.

■ What Is Your Message?

What message do you need to communicate to your team and clients? When you think about your business, what do you want your employees, clients, and the market to see, hear, and feel about your message?

Whatever your answers are to those questions, you will need to embody and deliver this message long before others will. You must communicate your message every day. Multiple times a day. And remember, the delivery won't always be through your words.

You can deliver that message even more effectively through your actions, your integrity, your kindness, your courage, and in many other ways. The key is to determine that message and communicate that message multiple times every single day in many ways.

There are three pieces to a clear leadership message: Your values, your vision, and your conviction.

In previous chapters, we've talked about values and vision. Please visit those sections in chapters 3 and 8 to develop your values and vision statement if you haven't already.

Conviction may seem odd to mention here, but conviction is the energy in which you stand behind the values and vision that you are communicating. Think of a leader that truly believes in their service, the speaker that rouses the crowd, or a preacher that gets the congregation standing. What is it that separates them from the ordinary?

It is the conviction of their communication. It becomes contagious. When you embody your message's values, vision, and conviction, you move people and that's a good thing. Martin Luther King, Jr. represented all three aspects of this idea. Winston Churchill, Mother Teresa, Nelson Mandela, and Abraham Lincoln are also great examples of leaders with conviction.

Your conviction comes out in your body language, tone of voice, and confidence. BLUE Shirt Leaders are aware of the power of conviction and use these aspects of communication to create an energy and excitement around their ideas and ideals. Sharing your excitement about where your business is going is not only good for your team, but it's good for your customers and YOU.

Many organizations post vision statements and values on plaques or in various other places to get the message in front of people. That's a good start. But just like goals, you need to help employees have a relationship with the most important messaging in your business.

Ultimately, these key messages need to be part of your mindsets, habits, and communication. I worked for one organization where we would say the mission of the organization every week together. In another, the values were on our ID cards.

Other things you need to communicate are expectations, goals, successes, failures, opportunities, etc. These messages also must be shared clearly and consistently. In this way, you're going beyond just words and conveying the significance of your message to those you lead and serve.

When it comes to communication, here are ten things your employees want you to do:

1. Put people first, listen, and be responsive to employee needs.
2. Stay true to the mission, vision, and values.
3. Hold others and yourself accountable.
4. Consistently and early on, communicate changes or adjustments.
5. Give recognition and praise to employees.
6. Create a safe space for mistakes and taking risks.
7. Lead up, down, and sideways.
8. Be consistent in how you lead.
9. Be honest and sincere with tact.
10. Provide feedback, mentorship, and training (i.e., resources).

This list is designed to get you thinking about what those you lead want from you. Now you get to decide how to communicate these things.

■ A Question To Ponder

Take the next five minutes to think about the items on the previous list and then answer the question: How can I communicate what's on this list in my words, actions, energy, and the culture as a whole?

The more thorough and nuanced your communication with your team, the easier it will be for them to perform at their best. When you communicate well and embody the message, your team is empowered with clarity of purpose and direction. Next, they'll need the resources to act.

The Resources Habit

When I ran Thousand Hills Pet Resort, we constantly needed new dog leashes, suitable food containers, and water hoses. If you've ever walked a dog on a leash or used a water hose around dogs, you know they love to bite them.

It was a rare day that a dog didn't chew a leash through, or a hose didn't get a new bite mark on it. I remember walking out into the chain-link yards filled with brightly colored play toys (think big plastic tables, slides, barrels, etc.), watching the dogs run around, and then noticing a broken leash or three on the ground.

Since we didn't allow the dogs to play with their collars on, for fear of dogs getting their mouths caught in a collar and causing a big issue, we used rope-like leashes that looped around the dogs' necks. These brightly colored leash remnants would be scattered all over the boarding area.

On any day, you could walk out to daycare or boarding and find a hose squirting water in various directions, including directly at the kennel host because of the newest bite.

We needed leashes and hoses to take care of the dogs. We also needed good food storage to prevent any critters from getting to the food in our barn. To be profitable as a business, we needed to have an abundance of these resources.

If we lacked leashes, it slowed down the whole process of getting a dog into the yards. The lack of leashes could severely hamper our whole system and create customer service issues, safety issues, and more.

The broken hoses caused difficulties with keeping the dogs cool and giving them water without soaking the hosts. With a shortage of working hoses, we had to drag hoses across the facility, wasting precious time.

When I talk about resources, remember they come in a few categories. These include people, materials/supplies, and technology. If computers go down, many businesses are screwed. If people are too busy to meet and collaborate, the business suffers. If your supply chain gets disrupted, an entire system grinds to a halt (COVID has revealed this reality all too clearly).

The list goes on and on for what can go wrong when needed resources are not available. What resources does your business need? How are you helping your team get what they need to perform at their best?

Too often, employees came to me frustrated because we didn't have any leashes. After this happened several times, it became standard for us to order fifty extra leashes once a month. Why? Not only to aid employees in performing the job better but to show employees we were listening and responding to their needs. Eventually, better leashes were found, and the need to order extras disappeared.

■ Questions To Ponder

Take the time to put in writing a list of the primary resources your employees need. Begin with the technological resources required. What would you have if you could magically supply employees with the ideal tech resources?

Then focus on the physical items needed to run the business. What are you not providing that you know would be ideal for your team to have?

Finally, who are the people your business needs? Some people to surround yourself with include people who are detail-oriented, sales-focused, innovative, proactive, collaborative, etc.

When I was working at the pet resort, I could dial in our technology and materials resources reasonably quickly. It was the people resource that was the hardest. That's where the next habit comes in.

The Delegation Habit

Delegating responsibility means giving your team control over what they are responsible for. When you delegate responsibility instead of tasks, employees have the power to make decisions without your input. This habit raises the limits of what they can do in your business. Employees can innovate, be courageous, and work together in ways they would never have. BLUE Shirt Leaders give their employees the stage and watch the magic.

Often, a business owner will explain the duties, do some training, share a checklist, and then head off to do their work. Weeks go by, and the business owner notices an error or two and goes to figure out what's going on.

Meanwhile, the new employee is trying their best but is perplexed about what to do when issues arise. They've attempted to follow the owner's instructions, but they struggle and fail because they can't recall everything they learned during those brief training sessions. This leads to a lack of productivity, mistakes, frustration, and lower employee engagement.

When the owner finally comes out of their office, everything is raised to the level of "catastrophe" to them. They're now even busier than they were before, attempting to clean up the mess. This putting-out-fires system of leadership repeats until the new employee develops a good process or is terminated and replaced by someone who will almost certainly have the same experience and make the same mistakes.

This catastrophe response cycle happens when an owner doesn't delegate responsibility or responsibly!

■ My First Lunch at Alpha Academy

On my first day of work at the Alpha Academy, Jack, the president of the program, took me to lunch. This lunch would be one of the first of several hundred we had together during eight years of working together.

I don't remember where we ate, but over that meal, he shared the full story of how the program started, what he saw in me and what he expected, and how they do things in a general sense, along with his availability. Additionally, he had lots of questions about my life experiences and ambitions.

Jack was laying the foundation of responsibility for my role. He was emphasizing how important I was to the program, how much he cared, and how much the program meant to him. This meeting set the stage for me to take the job more seriously than before.

If you go back to the list in the over-communication section, I think you'll see that Jack covered most of the checkpoints on the list in this one lunch. Jack's approach was empowering, and he was setting me up for success.

The conversations we had over the years built a high level of trust and allowed me to make decisions without asking Jack so many questions. It helped me take responsibility for my decisions (even when they didn't work out). It also boosted my desire to be innovative and develop new ideas.

Hiring someone and delegating duties to them is easy and can be done in a few hours or days. Hiring and training someone on your systems, values, and vision takes purposeful intention and time spent with them. When you do this, you've now delegated *responsibilities* to them.

When Jack did this with me, I began to embody the Alpha Academy values. I understood the bigger vision of impacting lives for generations. My perspective shifted from being an employee to an "owner" of my role and duties. I was fully "bought in." I was committed. To go back to our three frogs on the log story, I made it to the lily pad!

Ownership happens when you help your employees take responsibility for their role. But it starts with YOU taking responsibility for your part and not doing everyone else's work (see chapter 1). It means you use the mindsets and habits mentioned in previous chapters to become a BLUE Shirt Leader.

■ Simple Steps to Delegate Responsibility

Use the acronym CORA to help you remember how to delegate, which stands for Communicate, Obstacles, Resources, and Accountability/Actions.

Communicate:
Determine what needs to be communicated to whom and by when. Additionally, communicate expectations and desired outcomes.

Obstacles:
Discuss potential obstacles and strategies to overcome these obstacles.

Resources:
Share available resources the employee has access to and how to engage these resources.

Accountability:
Determine a plan for follow-up and specific timelines employees will be accountable for.

During follow-up conversations, it is helpful to apply the CORA process.

If you delegate responsibility well, you will have a team of dedicated, bought-in, and committed employees. You will have a team who will love to follow your systems, collaborate, and have the integrity to work at the highest standards. These team members will genuinely enjoy working under your leadership house, and you can trust them to do their work well.

It is only fitting that we end the mindsets and habits section of this book by focusing on celebration. The celebration habit is simple and does wonders for employee morale.

The Celebration Habit

My favorite memory of working at Thousand Hills Pet Resort was our summer employee party. I still have a picture of me with water splashing up around my face and body as I slid down this one-hundred-foot black Slip 'N Slide in the middle of the farmhouse front lawn.

The party was a celebration of our work. It was a celebration of the team growing and our financial numbers growing. But it was mostly a celebration of the people who worked there and demonstrated our value of "fun."

That was a banner day for me. I believe it was for several of the employees as well. We had great BBQ, played on the huge water slide, and had tons of fun. That day, we took the habit of celebration to a new level.

I have a client who owns an architectural firm and does quarterly hiking, backpacking, or biking trips with his team to develop connections and celebrate their successes. They also do an annual BBQ and retreat where they focus on the upcoming year's company goals and personal goals. I had an opportunity to participate in this year's retreat and it was a lot of fun.

We've all heard of organizations taking their entire team on a trip to an island, a resort, or a retreat to thank them for their hard work. Other companies include gift certificates to restaurants or a spa to thank their significant others, along with various gifts as simple as a coffee card or birthday card.

The ways to celebrate your employees are endless. Unfortunately, most businesses don't celebrate success enough. They get too busy and think annual reviews are good enough.

While employers put celebration as a low priority, employees put knowing they are seen and appreciated at the top of the list. Here's a list of quirky ways you can celebrate success AND the risks people on your team take.

Yes, you read that right, *risks*. Rare is the employer that celebrates the risky actions and mistakes of their employees. Why is this? Doesn't leading well require risks? The BLUE Shirt Leader is different. They celebrate the risks their team members take. As I mentioned in chapter 6 and throughout this book, these leaders understand that if their team is going to be truly empowered, they also must be allowed to take risks and screw up from time to time.

Ten Ways To Celebrate:

1. Provide lunch onsite or offsite.
2. Play a game in which everyone gets to win something.
3. Recognize them on social media.
4. Pull them aside and thank them specifically for something they did.
5. Bring them their favorite coffee or treat.

6. Compose a hand-written note and leave it on their desk.

7. Put a celebratory message on a t-shirt.

8. Provide gift cards to the employee's favorite restaurant, store, or coffee shop.

9. Give people an extra day off.

10. Provide a day off so employees can attend a sporting event, take a spa day, or enjoy a recreation day.

But what about celebrating failures? Surely you don't want to throw a lunch for the team to celebrate failures, right? Well, not so fast. An empowering BLUE Shirt Leader celebrates successes and highlights the risks and failures that got the team there.

When risks taken ultimately led to a huge win or breakthrough, it's important to acknowledge that without the failures and risks, the team would not be where they are. One way to show appreciation for mistakes is to highlight the original failure(s) that led to the success you are celebrating. Approaching a celebration in this way creates a culture of empowerment.

Lunch or any other number of options may be in order to celebrate a smart risk that ended in failure. When a team member tries something risky to earn a client or goes out on a limb with an idea that doesn't work out, you can write them a note to celebrate their courage (see chapter 8). Sometimes what appears like a huge mistake ends up being a huge win where the timing was just wrong. Sometimes, we need to celebrate courage to try, not just the win.

Celebrating your team's mistakes or miscues is possibly just as important as celebrating the wins. The message should always be about belief in the person and focus on the intention behind the risk taken. When business owners ignore or squash the ideas and attempts of their employees, they crush the empowering spirit of celebration.

■ The Critical COO

The COO of a business I worked for decided it was time for her to come out of her office and criticize the team's work. Not evaluate, not support, but straight-out criticize. This was her stated goal.

As the assistant director at a senior living facility, part of my responsibilities was to flip the rooms after a resident left. The facility had a lot of empty rooms because of poor performance in the sales team, people passing away, and employee turnover.

When I started working there, I did several things. I replaced the head chef for the facility, hired a new activities coordinator, and in partnership with the facilities manager, we began reducing the long list of maintenance issues.

Contracts were cleaned up and we were having more tours than ever before. Last, the care staff was beginning to sync, and we had some continuity developing. All these improvements occurred within the first three months of my employment.

When the COO came in, she wanted to "walk the facility." During her walk through, she criticized every crack, dust particle, and misplaced napkin. It was indeed a sight to behold to hear this lady point out everything we did wrong.

When we reached a room on the third floor, everything fell apart. The fridge had a smudge on it, a wall needed painting, and a closet door needed to be put back on the hinges. The facility manager had removed the door to accommodate an oversized washer and dryer. The extra effort and service to the residents were lost on the COO.

The CEO was with her, and as we stepped out, she mumbled to him how stupid we were and wondered aloud why we couldn't just figure this out. This was only one of several ugly encounters with her over my six months working there.

It wasn't too much longer before I gave notice and walked away from that job. The problem wasn't the criticism. I can take reasonable criticism. Even the "stupid" comment wasn't that big of a deal.

The problem was the lack of acknowledgment of the successful hires and system improvements that had been made. The COO made no celebration of progress. There was no end in sight for the criticism and abuse.

■ Celebrate and Recognize the Good and Bad

When business owners fail to recognize the hard work of their employees, whether it's a miss or a success, they have failed. If an employee consistently struggles to perform at work, the business owner has failed. The owner hasn't appropriately communicated, trained, or systematized their business effectively to get their desired results. The owner has failed to empower their team, not the other way around.

But when a small business owner embodies the empowerment pillar of the BLUE Shirt Leadership Framework, then loyalty, consistency, and efficiency from their employees follow. When that leader is also self-aware, remains accountable, and chooses a growth mindset, their Leadership House will be full.

■ Conclusion

Learning how to make each one of your employees an excellent dance partner is paramount to your ability to empower your team and organization. It starts with *studying* your employees and understanding their knowledge, skills, and abilities, then utilizing these talents.

When you empower your team, you must provide clear and constant *communication*. Whether you are planning and choreographing something new or in the middle of a big project, communicating the big vision and values and understanding their style is necessary for outstanding performance.

None of this will work out if you don't consistently provide the *resources* of people, technology, and supplies they need to succeed with you and each other.

Next, open the door to help them understand what it means to work for your business. Help your employees see the stage they are now standing on and who is watching. They need to know what they are *responsible* for. Give them your attention and your intentions to help them become responsible.

Finally, no matter what happens, *celebrate* the wins and the losses. It's impossible to always have a perfect performance. Celebrate the efforts made as well as the successes.

When you empower your team in this way, they will want to keep dancing in your leadership house and perform at their best. As we wrap up this last pillar, you may say to yourself, "So far this has been great. You've shared some stories, metaphors, mindsets, and habits, and that's all good, but how do I put everything into practice?"

Don't worry, in the following chapters I will put all this together and show you how to implement the BLUE Shirt Leadership Framework into your life and business using a simple process that won't be overwhelming. After all, the last thing you need is another item on your to-do list that creates unnecessary stress!

To get there, you'll learn the six-step process to implementation and how I personally use the framework. In the final chapter is a simple ten-day guide to jumpstart your progress toward becoming a BLUE Shirt Leader.

Ready to supercharge your results with the BLUE Shirt Leadership Framework? Don't wait! Apply now for a consultation with Kyle Gillette and receive personalized guidance to fast-track your success. Take the first step towards transformative leadership.

SCAN HERE

Chapter 11:

Implementing the BLUE Shirt
Leadership Framework

In the story of the three little pigs, we have an excellent metaphor for building a leadership house that will stand against the winds of change, the pounding of the market, and the whims of employees, customers, and competition. But only a leadership house built with care over time will stand up to the barrage of challenges faced by every leader and organization.

Right now, I bet there are probably several wolves huffing and puffing trying to disrupt your business and your leadership. Their attacks are likely affecting your thinking and confidence. One thing I know for sure is that there will be a lot of huffing and puffing in these next several months as you transition yourself and your organization to the BLUE Shirt Leadership model.

Communication challenges, priority disruptions, and market shifts are just a few of the threats likely coming your way. However, as you build and reinforce your BLUE Shirt Leadership House, the internal and external threats of the big bad wolf won't be able to stop you from accomplishing what you want.

If you follow the mindsets and habits in this book, they will help lay the foundation, build upon the foundation, and improve your leadership house. Each mindset and habit serve a specific purpose for achieving business growth and long-term success.

Before we break down this process, please know that you don't need to implement all the mindsets and habits within the Framework at once. Start by leaning on the mindsets and habits you already use, leverage your strengths, and manage your weaknesses.

The BLUE Shirt Leadership Framework is not one massive jumble of things you need to unwind and get into your leadership agenda immediately. Instead, implementing the framework is systematic, simple, and sane. It takes time to add everything to your leadership toolbox, but the changes, when implemented consistently over time, will be worth the effort.

BLUE Shirt Leaders know that becoming the leaders they are meant to be is an ongoing and fantastic experience. As you embark on a more purposeful journey to grow your leadership, I promise the rewards you experience and the influence you gain will shape a legacy of leadership that lasts.

I want you to picture your Leadership House today.

- What does it look like?
- How strong is the foundation?
- Are there nails needing to be re-secured?
- Do you need to reinforce some walls?
- How does that front door look?
- How is your curb appeal?

Many leaders and business owners haven't given the attention their leadership house deserves. Things may be a little rundown and some basic maintenance might be order, or maybe it's time for a complete renovation. Fortunately, you have the repair manual in your hand along with all the tools you will need to build a very different leadership house for the future of your business and yourself.

■ "This Is Going to Take Too Much Time"

Some of you may be thinking, "This seems like it's going to take a lot of time and effort." You're right. However, the time commitment isn't what you think it is. Implementing this process and framework into your life and leadership takes a focused effort of only ten to fifteen minutes per day. Trust me, I know! I have worked with hundreds of leaders, and they have seen significant changes with just fifteen minutes a day of focused effort.

Here's why the time commitment isn't as big as you think.

The beauty of this process is that you can use the power of your unconscious mind. As you work on these behaviors and utilize phone reminders to keep you on track, your unconscious mind will naturally guide you along the way.

You're creating new pathways in your brain to help you adjust mindsets and habits to that of a BLUE Shirt Leader. I shared in the section on neurocycling that you are leveraging your brain's neuroplasticity by engaging your conscious and unconscious mind in this change process.

The best part is that your unconscious will do the lion's share of the work. To reinforce all the changes in your thought patterns and behaviors, you will simply need to commit to just ten to fifteen minutes per evening.

As a guide to your writing, record thoughts on what went well, what you learned, and what you will do differently next time for each prompt. It's simple and quick, but the impact is enormous.

The key to the process is that you record your performance late in the evening, which will enable your unconscious to work on any "problems" while you sleep! And because you have set aside time for this reporting and feedback, you allow yourself to think more reflectively and purposefully about the chosen areas.

As I've said hundreds of times on my podcast and to clients,

I want to help you make small shifts in your habits and mindsets today that will create massive change for your future.

That future is one where you are becoming the leader you're meant to be! Here's how.

Implementing the Mindsets and Habits of the BLUE Shirt Leadership Framework

It's critical to start any growth practice with a goal in mind. To assist you in determining which habits and mindsets to focus on first, I've provided a six-step process.

There are twenty mindsets and twenty habits in this framework. At first glance, that may seem to be an overwhelming amount to learn and implement. Fortunately, each of these mindsets is intuitive. They build on each other and synergize with one another in a way that makes them easy to incorporate.

Neuroscientist, author, and thirty-year researcher on how our brains work, Dr. Caroline Leaf, teaches it takes sixty to ninety days to detox negative patterns. To keep it simple, I'm suggesting you work in ninety-day increments while focusing on only four mindsets/habits at a time.

■ The Implementation Steps

The first step to developing your BLUE Shirt Leadership transformation is from the accountability pillar or the habit of commitment. Take a moment right now to commit to developing your leadership skills. Commitment is the foundational step in implementing this robust growth practice for your leadership.

Next, review the habits and mindsets summarized below. Take your time to note which habits and mindsets you already have down. Then reference your notes and the areas you highlighted in this book to help you decide which four to focus on. I strongly recommend choosing at least three that you excel in, building these strengths to incredible levels, and choosing one that you would like to develop.

Next, add these habits and mindsets to a journal to track your daily progress. Then set up your phone to alert you with three or four reminders throughout the day to think about these specific habits and/or mindsets. This will help you to be more aware of the progress you are making.

Then start telling people—via phone, email, and text. Tell at least fifteen people that you have made a commitment to grow as a leader, then share the areas you are focusing on and invite them to join you.

Repeat this process as you work through the mindsets and habits that fit your strengths best. This approach ensures that you've allowed your mind ample time to embed the new mindset or habit into your life and leadership.

After repeating this process over several months, you will be WELL on your way to becoming the BLUE Shirt Leader you are meant to be!

I want to emphasize that it is best to start by focusing on the mindsets and habits you are doing well with and leave the areas that are not within your strengths for other people on your team to excel in.

For example, I am not an innovative leader. I need outside help with this area of leadership. Maybe it's because I can be cautious about the risks I'm willing to take with my business. Trying to become a superhero-level innovative leader isn't a fit for me, but I understand the value of innovation and want this in my business.

My best solution is to find someone on my advisory board or team that can push me a little and pull me forward and that I trust not to drive me off the cliff! I've also hired coaches in the past who work with me on building confidence in innovation.

Maybe you're not the rah-rah, motivational leader type, but your organization needs this. Simply communicate the vision in a way that fits your style and encourage team members that excel in the spotlight to drum up some motivation.

Perhaps listening isn't your strongest skill. Find other ways for people to provide you feedback so that they feel heard. This doesn't mean you get a pass on improving your listening. It just means there may be different ways to create effective communication that don't require you to sit down and listen to someone for thirty minutes straight.

As much as you may want to be good at all forty of these habits and mindsets, no one can be, and it isn't worth trying. After all, part of being a successful BLUE Shirt Leader is allowing others to excel.

■ Journal Practice Steps

1. Commit to focusing on four areas of your leadership development for ninety days.

2. Review the mindsets and habits in the list below.

3. Set up three or four daily reminders to remind you to think about the mindset or habit you've chosen to help you maintain consistent focus and growth.

4. Tell several people about what you are doing and ask them to help hold you accountable for doing your daily log.

5. Do the daily work of journaling.

6. Repeat the cycle with a new set of four every ninety days.

Self-Awareness Mindsets and Habits Summarized

Values Mindset: I filter my business and leadership decisions and actions through my personal and professional values.

Humble Mindset: I think of myself less and focus on others. Growing others is growing myself.

Patience Mindset: I will slow down to speed up and become patient with myself and all other stakeholders.

Trusting Mindset: I trust my strengths and those of others, along with the systems and processes we've developed.

Observant Mindset: I leverage the power of the three v's of communication and my intuition.

Platinum Habit: I treat others the way they want to be treated.

Intuitive Habit: I listen to and trust my intuition as a decision-making tool.

Writing Habit: I use the power of writing/journaling to help me become more self-aware.

Silence Habit: I intentionally slow down to observe or reflect as I go through the many transitions of the day.

Coachee Habit: I am committed to working with a coach or mentor to develop my leadership and business.

Accountability Mindsets and Habits Summarized

Goals Mindset: I act on what needs to get done in a systematic and measurable way.

Responsibility Mindset: I choose to be the one who is ultimately responsible and able to respond.

Integrity Mindset: I am true to my word as a cornerstone of my leadership.

Priorities Mindset: I maintain focus on the most important items in my business.

Systems Mindset: I remain open to changes in order to improve my business systems.

Passive Accountability Habit: I build accountability by sharing my goals, dreams, and vision.

Active Accountability Habit: I schedule and welcome weekly accountability with partners.

Structures Habit: I use the power of digital tools and analog measures to maintain accountability.

Self-Commitment Habit: I take action on decisions.

Advisory Board Habit: I seek the advice of a group of five to seven leaders as a means of support and growth.

Growth Mindsets and Habits Summarized

Risk Mindset: I courageously take smart or intuitive risks that can lead to failure or success.

Learner Mindset: I choose to learn from failures and successes.

Persistent Mindset: I persist despite failure, fatigue, and frustration.

Abundance Mindset: I believe opportunities abound.

Sales Mindset: I remember I am selling much more than just our products and services as the leader.

Focus Habit: I focus on staying on target with what I am trying to achieve, both short term and long term.

Calibration Habit: I gladly evaluate my performance against the greats inside and out of my industry.

Feedback Habit: I consistently give and receive feedback from stakeholders.

Listening Habit: I choose to listen deeply to people inside and outside my organization to gather insight.

Practice Habit: I work on the fundamentals of what makes me and my business successful.

Empowerment Mindsets and Habits Summarized

Kindness Mindset: I am continuously developing a caring, friendly, and fun culture.

Courageous Mindset: My willingness to accept and adapt to changes is evident.

Collaborative Mindset: Unifying my team toward a common goal and purpose is my mission.

Innovative Mindset: I openly encourage curiosity and questions and am willing to try new things and think outside the box.

Coaching Mindset: I am intentional about conversations and seek to discover new insights and awareness through the power of questions and deep listening.

Study Habit: I stay curious about what makes my team tick and then leverage their strengths.

Over-Communication Habit: I am not afraid to share my leadership vision, values, and conviction.

Resources Habit: I provide the tools, training, and resources my team needs to succeed.

Delegation Habit: I am excited about giving people authority over their areas of strength.

Celebration Habit: I celebrate the people I lead in their successes and failures.

SELF-AWARENESS	
Values Mindset	Platinum Habit
Humble Mindset	Intuitive Habit
Patience Mindset	Writing Habit
Trusting Mindset	Silence Habit
Observant Mindset	Coachee Habit

ACCOUNTABILITY

Goals Mindset	Passive Habit
Responsibility Mindset	Active Habit
Integrity Mindset	Structures Habit
Priorities Mindset	Self-Commitment Habit
Systems Mindset	Advisory Board Habit

GROWTH

Risk Mindset	Focus Habit
Learner Mindset	Calibration Habit
Persistent Mindset	Feedback Habit
Abundance Mindset	Listening Habit
Sales Mindset	Practice Habit

EMPOWERMENT

Kindness Mindset	Study Habit
Courageous Mindset	Over-Communication Habit
Collaborative Mindset	Resources Habit
Innovative Mindset	Delegation Habit
Coaching Mindset	Celebration Habit

Chapter 12:

How I Implement the BLUE Shirt Leadership Framework

I'm always disappointed when I read business or self-help books that don't include how the author implements their ideas. To help you avoid the same disappointment or frustration, I want to share my approach to implementing the BLUE Shirt Leadership Framework.

This is not "the" approach, but more how I do it and how it has evolved to fit into my leadership. For some people, my approach might be a great template. For others, it might need a bit of adjusting. I have italicized the habits and mindsets so you can see how they fit into my life. Notice, I don't cover all of them.

My alarm goes off every morning at 5:28 a.m. I chose this time because it makes "I get up at 5:30 a.m." true. If I'm going to encourage other people to be impeccable with their word (chapter 5), I'd better work hard to do that myself. "Get up" in my world means awake and moving, not slapping at the alarm clock.

Getting up at this time provides ninety minutes of prep time before starting the day. The first forty-five minutes are the most important. Here's how I use the first forty-five minutes to maintain the BLUE Shirt Leadership approach.

■ Your First Forty-Five

I have a client that is a real estate firm owner, and he is developing a morning routine. He understands that if he can own the first forty-five minutes of his morning, he can own the rest of his day.

So far, implementing a routine has been a bit of a struggle. If you don't already have a morning routine, it may be difficult for you too! But that's okay. All change requires some level of struggle.

A simple internet search will bring up scores of articles discussing the importance of the first five to fifty minutes of your day. A Harvard study suggests ten minutes, an article on Medium suggests fifteen minutes, and in the book Miracle Morning, author Hal Elrod suggests sixty minutes. If I can get forty-five minutes, I'm golden. But there are many mornings where ninety minutes are possible, and I use them all.

For the sake of this book, I propose aiming for forty-five minutes because you will feel pressured if you try to get everything done with less time than this.

■ My Forty-Five-Minute Start

☑ I drink a big glass of water, eight ounces or more.

☑ I get comfortable on the couch or in my chair and pray/meditate for about ten to twenty minutes (silence habit.)

☑ I then read the Bible for fifteen to twenty minutes (learner mindset).

☑ Then I do my Spanish lesson for ten minutes.

☑ I end by watching a few minutes of a YouTube educational video if I have time.

This routine takes about forty-five minutes. If there's extra time, I'll watch YouTube or read a book to learn something about my industry or one of my client's industries. I rarely exercise in the morning. Many people swear by exercising in the morning, but that just does not work for me. If it works for you, by all means, do it. I do CrossFit in the evenings or afternoons, three days a week.

The important thing is to create a consistent routine that gets your mind and body going.

My Morning Work Routine

After my first forty-five self-care routine, I have different work routines depending on the day of the week. Mondays start with a CEO meeting to help me prepare for the week. My "CEO" meeting is a thirty-minute meeting with the Big Guy upstairs to ensure my priorities are aligned and to seek advice, pray for feedback, and listen.

Every other Tuesday, I meet with an accountability partner to discuss life and for us to hold each other accountable for the personal commitments we've made. These meetings have been happening for over four years and seem to work well for us.

Additionally, there's a networking leader group meeting every Tuesday to help calibrate business progress, collaborate with other professionals, and practice sales and speaking skills.

Every other Wednesday, I meet with my mentor. This mentor meeting helps me build a more successful marriage and business. On Wednesdays, I also run a mastermind group where a few entrepreneurs and I talk about our successes and the risks we want to take, and then challenge one another to grow our businesses. No topic is off-limits.

Thursday mornings are open. But they can typically get filled with coaching calls.

Friday mornings, I go to my Toastmasters group to practice my speaking (over-communication habit) and listening skills. The rest of Friday is spent reviewing and updating my financial and time budget and wrapping up my work week. I need to monitor my financial and time budget to help keep my priorities on track.

Typical Workdays

During the typical workday, one of my favorite habits to use is the habit of silence. This habit creates centeredness and focus. It also locks in self-awareness and allows me to operate withing the Leadership Framework throughout the day. As described in chapter 4, you can use transition moments to move in and out of silence throughout your workday.

Besides the coaching calls and various administrative tasks for my business, I record coaching calls and participate in classes to become more self-aware of communication tendencies and to grow my coaching and leadership skills.

Beyond the appointments and morning accountability meetings, my Saturday routine mentioned below helps me maintain accountability to the big picture for my life and business and provides feedback on the details.

For maintaining a growth mindset, attending a bi-weekly mastermind is a significant boost, as are any classes I take.

One habit that was a challenge was choosing to put away devices and stop and listen to my family. It has been a significant growth point for me and my relationships.

My clients challenge me daily to maintain a growth mindset in part because I challenge them to do the same.

Maintaining an empowerment mindset is the most challenging. Although I collaborate with clients daily, there is room for me to grow. The most effective way I use this empowerment mindset is by studying the assessments I have my clients and employees take to understand them better.

I try to find people and resources to serve my clients and empower them in ways I know I can't. Finally, I find that having open coaching-like conversations with my employees and with the vendors I work with helps empower them too.

How Do I Leverage the BLUE Shirt Leadership Framework on Weekends?

Saturday is one of my favorite days of the week, not only because I get to play, hike, bike, work around the yard, and be with my wife and kids, but also because I get to reflect on the past week and look forward to the next. On Sundays, as a family we do chores, fun activities, and church.

Let me go back to Saturday because I want to encourage you to follow my lead on this. My Saturday reflection time is one of my week's most rewarding and essential times.

Every Saturday, I complete my weekly review. After my first forty-five, I do five different things to end the week and start the following week well.

- ☑ Complete my first forty-five minutes of focusing on my BLUE Shirt Leadership development.
- ☑ Complete a weekly review (see below).
- ☑ Work through my MOLO questions (see chapter 7).
- ☑ Review my triggers list (see below).
- ☑ Finally, I review my goals, values, mission, and vision statements.

■ Weekly Review

My weekly review looks at the meetings and tasks of the previous week. I record my meetings into specific color-coded categories in a time log to ensure I stay focused and hit my goals. I track the hours I spend in seven categories, ensuring I progress toward all my personal and professional goals. You can look at my categories in the resources section on the website by visiting blueshirtcoaching.com/book-resources.

Looking back over the week often reminds me of the progress made (celebration habit) and items I need to address. Next, I look forward and check my to-do list and upcoming meetings for the week ahead. The look forward helps prepare me for the week ahead and helps me catch things I may need to prepare for and maximize scheduled meetings. Periodically, I'll jump ahead a month or two as well.

About a year ago, I added the look-ahead step to help me keep my schedule under control and prevent doubling up meetings. The weekly review only takes ten minutes to complete but is invaluable.

■ Complete a MOLO

If you don't remember what the MOLO is, take a moment and review that section in chapter 7. The MOLO is my favorite part of the review. It's a personal feedback loop on habits and progress made that can elevate your success. I've been using MOLO as part of my system for over three years, and it's a joy to look back at all the things that started, stopped, and continued along my journey to where my business is today.

I typically choose a topic to focus on and spend ten to fifteen minutes working through the questions I provided in chapter 7 to get my head right and move things forward. I document my notes as a project within my Todoist application—more on Todoist in the systems section below.

■ Review a Triggers List

After the weekly review and MOLO are complete, it's on to the easy stuff. Built into my Todoist is a checklist of about sixty reminder items related to my business or personal life. When I read this checklist, it typically triggers me to add a few other things to my to-do list that I may have forgotten.

One week the triggers list focuses on personal items, and the following week, on professional. The professional list is divided into office, development, financial, client care, and marketing.

The trigger list is a list of things that are not top-of-mind items that I still want to achieve. After all, we are swamped, and things can slip through the cracks. A trigger list is a great way to ensure that doesn't happen. You can look at my list in the resources section on my website by visiting blueshirtcoaching. com/book-resources.

■ Fifty-Thousand-Foot Review: Calibration

Finally, I wrap up this time with a big-picture review. This big-picture review is a fifty-thousand-foot look at my life and my business. During this big-picture review time, I quickly review my top goals for the current year, the following year, then five years, and ten years.

Next, I take a moment and look at my vision, values, and mission. I read them aloud, just to anchor myself with them.

The fifty-thousand-foot review takes about five minutes to complete, and my Saturday review takes about thirty minutes. In addition to the first forty-five, you're still well within a ninety-minute window.

If you're like me, you also want to know the tools other business owners use to help them with their systems. Well, you're in luck. Here are my top seven tools.

My Top Seven Tools to Implement the BLUE Shirt Leadership Framework

I recently got off the phone with a prospect that didn't know how many hours she worked per week nor what communication tools to use, and she had no business goals. Yet, she is a top producer and runs a household full of kids and dogs. Imagine what would happen if she dialed in her systems!

Many people don't know how poor my memory can be at times. For twenty years, I believed my memory was terrible and that I could do nothing about it. Then I was introduced to the PDA. Do you remember that? The personal digital assistant. This device changed my life.

Nowadays, our sophistication with such devices has reached unreal levels, and I try to leverage these as much as I can. I use the following resources to help organize my life and business, helping me become a BLUE Shirt Leader.

- Google Workspace
- Calendly
- Todoist
- Apple Notes
- Notability
- Zoom
- Loom

I use a variety of other programs, but if I lost any of these seven, it would be devastating. These tools are critical to my daily leadership and business.

Before you read on, take the time to write down your top five to seven tools and briefly describe how you use them. Ask yourself if you could leverage these tools more effectively or efficiently.

■ Leverage Tools Through Systems

When possible, ensure your tools and resources are highly scalable. Remember, this list of tools is what I see as virtually irreplaceable for implementing the BLUE Shirt Leadership Framework into my life and business—not necessarily the top tools for running a business.

■ Google Workspace

If you want to become a BLUE Shirt Leader, communication is vital. Finding a communication suite you can use and leveraging it as much as possible will create powerful efficiency and productivity for your team.

For me, that communication suite is Google Workspace. I don't care what you use. Just find a team communication tool and use it. I appreciate Google's Workspace because of the simplicity of sharing documents, ease of email, calendar functionality, and integrations with other Google and non-Google apps. You can do this through Microsoft Office as well. I just prefer Google.

Using a tool like Google Workspace simplifies and helps you organize all the communication between your clients, employees, and prospects. It's one of the more empowering tools for your business and BLUE Shirt Leadership journey. Check it out by visiting https://workspace.google.com/.

■ Calendly

If you are still wasting time emailing back and forth to schedule meetings. STOP IT NOW and get a scheduler app. I highly recommend Calendly, which costs between $8 and $16 per month.

Calendly integrates with my website, Google Workspace, and my podcast. Not only does it allow people to book a meeting and get immediate confirmation, but it sends meeting reminder emails and follow-up emails and redirects people to landing pages. This tool has helped me win clients because once someone does a podcast or networks with me, it links to my customer relationship management system and puts them into a drip (automated messaging) campaign.

Using a tool like Calendly empowers clients, employees, and prospects to connect with you and get inside your BLUE Shirt Leadership House. Visit https://calendly.com/ to check it out.

■ Todoist

I've already shared some ways I use Todoist throughout this book. In short, this tool is my second brain. It makes adding tasks simple with smart dates, recurring tasks, and other great features, including powerful integrations with Calendly and Google Workspace.

Todoist is my primary tool for structures (S in the accountability P.A.S.S). It's straightforward to use and keeps me organized and accountable.

When you use a to-do list tool, you automatically build accountability by setting reminders and due dates. The best part about Todoist is that you can dump all the tasks you repeatedly do each week into the system, and it will remind you to get them done. This frees your mind to focus on more important items. You can leverage it for self-awareness and growth, as I do through the power of my weekly review. My MOLO, goals, vision, and any tasks associated with helping me to develop my leadership are documented and easily referenced in this tool. Visit todoist.com to learn more.

■ Notability

Notability is a digital note-taking app used in conjunction with an Apple Pencil. You can use it for recording notes while on calls during meetings or reading a book. Notability serves as a catch-all for anything I need to write as I meet with people. Visit https://notability.com/ to learn more.

■ Zoom

Zoom can be a BLUE Shirt Leader's best friend for accountability and growth. With Zoom or any other video conference software, you can interact face-to-face with anyone, anywhere. These connections can help you be more accountable and help you grow.

You can use the Zoom tool (or one like it) to build and meet with one or more people on your advisory board simultaneously, no matter where in the world they are. Visit https://zoom.us/ to learn more.

■ Loom

My last tool is Loom. It's an asynchronous communication tool. Loom helps me to screen capture and record audio and video to share with clients, team members, and prospects. It saves hours and lets me get across what I'm trying to say in a short three-minute video instead of a long email.

I use this tool daily, saving me many hours and communication headaches. Visit https://loom.com/ to learn more.

Now that you know the steps I've used to implement the BLUE Shirt Leadership Framework, in the final chapter, I'll give you a ten-day BLUE Shirt Leader Jump Start Guide so that you can implement the BLUE Shirt Leadership Framework into your life.

This BLUE Shirt Leader Jump Start Guide, combined with some tips and tricks from the previous chapters, will help you get started strong and keep your momentum so that you can become the BLUE Shirt Leader you're meant to be.

Chapter 13:

Your First Ten Days

Starting anything new is both challenging and filled with uncertainty. I still remember the first few weeks of running my business. It was exciting, chaotic, and overwhelming. I had a list of things I thought I needed to do, another of what I was told I should do, and a list of what I was doing. Those first few days were full of so much excitement.

In retrospect, success wasn't as complex as I'd thought it would be. Most things aren't that complex when you break them down into small steps you can follow. That's what I want to do for you here. I will break down the first ten days of your BLUE Shirt Leadership journey into small steps you can easily follow.

Daily Actions

■ Day One

Tell several people about your commitment to become a BLUE Shirt Leader, the leader you're meant to be. Share with them a few habits or mindset shifts you will be making. The primary purpose of day one is to establish a mindset of accountability up front on your journey to BLUE Shirt Leadership.

■ Day Two

Get a journal or download a digital journal and add the four habits/mindsets you'd like to focus on. Then join our Facebook community, BLUE Shirt Business Community or the Dads in Business Alignable

Community, to get encouragement and inspiration for your BLUE Shirt Leadership journey. Day two is about building some structure for your journey.

■ Day Three

Set an alarm reminder on your watch or phone so that you can start using the power of transition moments. Start with a target of three to five times per day. For a refresher on this, see chapter 4. This will help you stay present in your growth and learning as you develop your BLUE Shirt Leadership.

■ Day Four

Create a list of ten people you want on your advisory board, then schedule a date and time you will reach out to each of these people. Check out the advisory board section in chapter 6 for implementing this practice. The role of an advisory board is not to make decisions for you but to provide a reservoir of knowledge, critical thinking, and analysis to help increase your confidence in the many choices you will make as a BLUE Shirt Leader.

■ Day Five

Write three SMART goals you would like to achieve in the next three to six months. As you develop your SMART goals, don't forget to review them with your advisory board. They may have the resources and connections you need to achieve your goals. The SMART goals overview can be found in chapter 5. Goals that are written are far more likely to be completed.

■ Day Six

Contact us to take a DISC assessment. By taking a DISC assessment, you gain more awareness of yourself and a better understanding of the four communication styles of the people you lead.

■ Day Seven

Implement the MOLO into your weekly routine. If you need a refresher, visit chapter 7. The MOLO will help you monitor your progress and create intentional actions toward becoming a BLUE Shirt Leader.

■ Day Eight

Sit down and meet one-on-one with the people you lead and ask them how you could be a better communicator, resource, and support to them. Here are a few questions you can ask:

- ➲ How can I be a better communicator with you?
- ➲ What do you need from me that I haven't been providing?
- ➲ In what ways can I better support you?

BLUE Shirt Leaders don't shy away from challenging conversations or the feedback it creates. In this step, you're announcing an intentional shift in your leadership approach and a willingness to adapt your leadership to your team.

■ Day Nine

Begin practicing the 80/20 rule as it relates to your communication. Listen 80 percent of the time when appropriate and talk 20 percent of the time. This method is explained in the section on developing the coaching mindset in chapter 9. BLUE Shirt Leaders recognize that listening will significantly impact those they lead more than telling. The 80/20 rule helps remind us of this.

■ Day Ten

Develop the practice of gratitude. You can develop this practice in conversations, when something gets fouled up, or by using a journal. You can simply take a moment and reflect or record your thoughts. This process is described in the abundance mindset section in chapter 7. When you develop a gratitude practice, you are providing the fuel necessary for an abundance mindset, which will help you become the leader you're meant to be.

Final Thoughts

The tools you use and the routines you follow in the weeks and months ahead will help you shift your leadership in significant ways. As you apply the BLUE Shirt Leadership Framework to your life and business, you will be building, remodeling, and reinforcing your BLUE Shirt Leadership House for whatever comes your way.

A wise person once said, "We're either going into a crisis, coming out of a crisis, or in a crisis." That big bad wolf won't ever stop huffing and puffing at your Leadership House, but with a BLUE Shirt Leadership mindset, habits, and tools and the support of this community, your Leadership House will stand.

There are thousands of business owners and leaders whose mindsets and habits have blocked them from giving all they have. That can change with this book and the many other tools available as part of the BLUE Shirt Leadership community.

I hope that your goals and dreams will become a reality and that you will impact thousands of lives, even millions, as you become a BLUE Shirt Leader. As you have seen from the stories shared, our legacy as leaders can shift this world in powerful ways if we will do the work. Sometimes all the work required is a simple change in a habit or a new perspective on a mindset to change someone's life and business.

The World's Greatest General

One more story for you.

Mark Twain told a story about a man searching for the world's greatest general. The man spent his life searching and could not find him. When he arrived in heaven, the man walked over to St. Peter and said, "I'm looking for the world's greatest general." St. Peter said, "I know, I know, we've been expecting you, and I have good news. If you look right over there, you will see the world's greatest general."

The man excitedly looked over and said, "That is not the world's greatest general. That man was a cobbler in my hometown!" St. Peter responded, "But had he been a general, he would have been the greatest general ever."

Did the cobbler know this? Did he know his potential? Like many, he may not have been aware of his potential. He may not have been aware of who he was meant to be.

Sometimes we need others to help us achieve at our highest levels. We need a guide. I hope I've served as a guide for you through this book.

Onward, my new friend! I wish you the greatest success as you become the BLUE Shirt Leader you're meant to be.

Ready to supercharge your results with the BLUE Shirt Leadership Framework? Don't wait! Apply now for a consultation with Kyle Gillette and receive personalized guidance to fast-track your success. Take the first step towards transformative leadership.

SCAN HERE

About The Author

Kyle Gillette is the founder and CEO of BLUE Shirt Business Coaching. His mission is to help leaders shift their mindsets and habits to become the leaders they are meant to be. After running four different businesses and seeing two of them succeed, Kyle knows what it's like to have businesses fail and succeed. Kyle has been a small business coach to dozens of companies and ran a men's mentoring program for three years. He believes that every company should have a culture of accountability and growth with leaders who are self-aware and empower their teams. He is especially passionate about helping business owners in the home-services and trades industries, as he grew up in a blue-collar family. When not working with his clients, Kyle is a sports and CrossFit enthusiast.

Well Done!

Before you close this book and put it on the shelf, if you found the message of this book compelling, please consider leaving a review on Amazon.

As an author, I appreciate nothing more than reading reviews on Amazon and other book sites from those who have enjoyed the message of this book.

Your review could be what inspires someone to discover BLUE Shirt Leadership: A 4-Part Framework for Today's Leader.

Thank you

Kyle Gillette

One More Thing

Congratulations on becoming a BLUE Shirt Leader.

Now let's put this knowledge to work serving others.

To take a deep dive into BLUE Shirt Leadership and the Blue Shirt Leader Framework visit
🌐 www.blueshirtcoaching.com

To hire Kyle Gillette as a coach, workshop leader, or speaker contact Kyle at
🌐 kyle@blueshirtcoaching.com

For discount bulk purchases of this book for your organization or conference, please email the publisher at
🌐 Info@SkinnyBrownDogMedia.com

Right Now Leadership: A 4-Part Framework for Today's Leader is available as a group coaching experience, workshops, or one-one coaching program.

References:

- Mitchell, Curtis (5 February 1961). "She Can Teach You To Read 2,500 Words a Minute!". Denton Record-Chronicle (Denton, TX). Family Weekly Sunday Supplement.

- Cirillo, Francesco. "The Pomodoro Technique (The Pomodoro)" (PDF). Retrieved 30 December 2018.

- Tracy, Brian. Eat That Frog!: 21 Great Ways to Stop Procrastinating and Get More Done in Less Time. 2nd ed. San Francisco, CA: Berrett-Koehler Publishers, 2007.

- Allen, David, 1945 December 28-. Getting Things Done : the Art of Stress-Free Productivity. New York :Viking, 2001

- McKinsey Global Survey: War for talent 2000," extensive research conducted 1997 to 2000; survey of more than 12,000 executives at 125 midsize and large companies.

- Achievers Survey, 2020 Engagement and Retention Report.

- Pennebaker, James W., Smyth, Joshua M., Opening Up by writing it Down: How expressive writing improves health and eases emotional pain, New York, NY: The Guliford Press, 2016.

- Biro, Brian D., Beyond Success: the 15 secrets to effective leadership and life based on legendary coach John Wooden's pyramid of success. Pygmalion Press, 1997.

Printed in the USA
CPSIA information can be obtained
at www.ICGtesting.com
LVHW020306141023
760911LV00055B/977

9 781957 506708